A Brief Sanskrit Glossary

A Brief Sanskrit Glossary

A Spiritual Student's Guide to Essential Sanskrit Terms

enlarged 2nd edition compiled by
Abbot George Burke
(Swami Nirmalananda Giri)

LIGHT of the SPIRIT
PRESS
CEDAR CREST, NEW MEXICO

Published by
Light of the Spirit Press
lightofthespiritpress.com

Light of the Spirit Monastery
P. O. Box 1370
Cedar Crest, New Mexico 87008
www.OCOY.org

Copyright © 2018 Light of the Spirit Monastery.
All rights reserved.

ISBN-13: 978-1-7325266-2-4
ISBN-10: 1-7325266-2-1

Library of Congress Control Number: 2018966780
Light of the Spirit Press, Cedar Crest, New Mexico

Second Edition 2018

BISAC Categories:
OCC021000   BODY, MIND & SPIRIT / Reference
REL032030   RELIGION / Hinduism / Sacred Writings

12222018

Contents

Preface vii	M 76
A 1	N 88
B 22	O 96
C 32	P 97
D 36	R 111
E 45	S 116
G 47	T 143
H 52	U 149
I 54	V 153
J 56	W 167
K 61	Y 168
L 73	

Free Meditation Guide 175
About the Author 176
Light of the Spirit Monastery 178
Reading for Awakening 179

Preface

It is very beneficial for students of Indian thought, of the Bhagavad Gita, the Upanishads, the Yoga Sutras of Patanjali, and other Indian scriptures and philosophical works to expand their vocabularies to include the sanskrit terms included in them. English books about these works often contain many untranslated sanskrit words because there are no concise English equivalents. This glossary contains full translations and explanations of many of the most commonly used sanskrit terms, and will help students of these spiritual treatises gain a fuller understanding in their studies.

We recommend four other dictionaries:

Yoga-Vedanta Dictionary by Swami Sivananda. Divine Life Society of South Africa

A Concise Dictionary of Indian Philosophy by John Grimes. State University of New York Press

Sanskrit Glossary of Yogic Terms by Swami Yogakanti. Yoga Publications Trust, Bihar, India

A Sanskrit Dictionary by John M. Denton. John M. Denton

A

Abhasavada: Doctrine holding that all creation is a reflection of the Supreme Reality.

Abhaya(m): "Without fear;" fearlessness; a state of steadfastness in which one is not swayed by fear of any kind.

Abheda: Non-difference; non-duality.

Abheda-ahamkara: The pure ego that identifies itself with Brahman or the Absolute.

Abhedananda, Swami: A direct disciple of Sri Ramakrishna, who spent many years traveling and teaching Vedanta and Yoga in America.

Abhimana: Egoism; conceit; attachment; I-sense; pride; the function of the ego; the delusion of "me" and "mine;" identification with the body.

Abhimani: One who has egoistic feeling.

Abhimata: Desired; favorite; attractive; agreeable, appealing; object of choice.

Abhinivesha: Clinging to earthly life; will to live; strong desire; false identification of the Self with the body or mind; an instinctive clinging to life and a dread of death.

Abhisheka(m): Bathing–the ritual pouring of various items over a sacred image or personage in homage and worship.

Abhyantara: Internal; inward.

Abhyasa: Sustained (constant) spiritual practice.

Abhyasa Yoga: Yoga, or union with God, through sustained spiritual practice.

Abhyasin: Yoga-practitioner.

Achala: Not moving; immovable; standing still; firm; steady; fixed, unwavering; without change.

Achamana: Sipping water from the hollowed palm of the hand; a preliminary simple rite connected with ritualistic worship.

Achara: 1) Immobile. 2) Right conduct; good behavior; custom; practice; external observance of established rules and laws; teaching.

Acharya: Preceptor; teacher; spiritual teacher/ guide; guru.

Achintya: Unthinkable; inconceivable; incomprehensible; inexplicable. A title of Brahman because the mind cannot conceive Its nature.

Achintya shakti: Inscrutable power ineffable force.

Achyuta: The indestructible; the unchanging; the imperishable one–a title of Krishna.

Adesha: A divine command from within the being; teaching, as is upadesha–teaching received while sitting near (upa).

Adhara: 1) "To support or prop;" support; substratum; body apparatus. In yoga, it means various places of the body where the attention is focussed for control, concentration, and meditation. 2) A reservoir of pranic energies, storage units for the energies that flow into the subtle bodies through the chakras, therefore often mistaken for a chakra.

Adharma: Unrighteousness; demerit, failure to perform one's proper duty; unrighteous action; lawlessness; absence of virtue; all that is contrary to righteousness (dharma).

Adhibhautika: Elemental.

Adhibhuta: Primal Being; pertaining to the elements; the primordial form of matter.

Adhidaiva: Primal God.

Adhidaivika: Pertaining, to the heaven or the celestial beings.

Adhikara: Authority; qualification; jurisdiction; prerogative; office; claim; privilege.

Adhikari(n): An eligible or qualified person; a worthy person. It implies both fitness and capability.

Adhimatra: The degree of vairagya when worldly enjoyment becomes a source of pain.

Adhishthana(m): Seat; basis; substratum; ground; support; abode; the body as the abode of the subtle bodies and the Self; underlying truth or essence; background.

Adhiyajna: Primal Sacrifice; Supreme Sacrifice.

Adhyatma: The individual Self; the supreme Self; spirit.

Adhyatmika: Adhyatmic; pertaining to the Self (Atman or Jivatman), individual and Supreme (Paramatman).

Adi: First, original, or primary.

Adi Purusha: The First or Original Purusha. See Purusha.

Adibhuta: Primal Being; Primal Element; Primordial Matter. Also: Supreme Being and Supreme Element.

Adidaiva: Primal God; Supreme God.

Adinath (Adi Nath): The first teacher of the Nath Panthi, or

Nath Yogi Sampradaya, usually believed to be Shiva himself.
Adishakti: Primal Power.
Aditattva: The first principle; Brahman; Mula Prakriti; the first element (of matter) next but one above akasha in the gradation of subtlety.
Aditi: Boundless; unbounded; "Infinite Mother"–the source of all the cosmic forms of consciousness from physical upwards; in Vedic cosmology: the mother of the gods.
Aditya: The sun; the Sun God.
Adityas: Solar deities, the greatest of which is Vishnu.
Advaita: Non-dualism; non-duality; literally: not [a] two [dvaita].
Advaita Nishtha: Establishment in the state of non-duality.
Advaita vada: The theory that Brahman is the only existence; monism; Vedanta.
Advaita Vedanta: The teaching that there is only One Reality (Brahman-Atman), as found in the Upanishads. Non-dualistic philosophy, especially that of Shankara.
Advaitic: Non-dual; having to do with the philosophy of Advaita (Non-Dualism).
Advaitin: A proponent of Advaita philosophy.
Advaitist: A proponent of Advaita philosophy.
Adwitiya: Without a second.
Adya: Primordial; original.
Adyasakti: The Primal Energy; Avyaktam. or Mula Prakriti.
Agama: Scripture; particularly scriptures dealing with the four topics of temple construction and the making of images, philosophy, meditation practice, and methods of worship.

Agamapaya/agamapayi: That which appears and disappears–comes and goes.

Agami karma: Karma produced by present action that will be experienced by the individual in the future.

Agastya: A sage and reputed seer of many hymns in the Rig Veda.

Aghora: Not terrifying (ghora); benevolent; a title of Shiva.

Aghora Pantha: An order or sect of worshippers of Shiva (Shaivites).

Agni: Fire; Vedic god of fire.

Agnihotra: "Fire offering;" a Vedic fire sacrifice.

Agrahya: Unfit to be taken; that which cannot be grasped; that which cannot be understood; Brahman.

Aguna: Without guna or quality.

Aham: I; I-awareness; the ego; the individual soul; self-consciousness; the pure inner Self.

Aham Brahmasmi: "I am Brahman." The Mahavakya (Great Saying) of the Brihadaranyaka Upanishad.

Ahamika: Egoism; Pride.

Ahamkara: See Ahankara.

Ahankara: Ego; egoism or self-conceit; the self-arrogating principle "I," "I" am-ness; self-consciousness.

Ahara: Food; object of senses; anything taken in by the senses.

Ahata: Natural sound.

Ahimsa: Non-injury in thought, word, and deed; non-violence; non-killing; harmlessness.

Ahuti: Oblation (poured into the fire in sacrifices).

Airavata: The white elephant of Indra that was produced by the churning of the ocean.

Aishwarya: Dominion, power; lordship; divine glory; majesty; splendor; attribute(s) of Ishwara.

Aja: Unborn; unproduced; birthless.

Ajapa Japa: A yogic term that means the natural, spontaneous sound of the breath that goes on perpetually through the simple act of breathing. This sound is extremely subtle, and though non-verbal is the highest form of mantra. The Mantra "So'ham" (I am He) which is produced by the breath itself, without any conscious effort at repeating it: the inhalation sounding 'So' and the exhalation 'ham.'

Ajapa Gayatri: So'ham Mantra.

Ajara: Without old age; ageless.

Ajara Amara Avinashi Atma: The ageless, immortal, imperishable Self.

Ajna chakra: "Command Wheel." Energy center located at the point between the eyebrows, the "third eye." The seat of the mind. The medulla center opposite the point between the eyebrows, having two "petals" or rays.

Ajnana: Ignorance; nescience.

Ajnani: One who is ignorant, devoid of knowledge and wisdom.

Akanksha: Desire (all round).

Akara: Form; shape; category.

Akarma: Inaction; non-doing.

Akarshana shakti: Power of attraction.

Akarta: Non-doer; non-attached.

Akasha: Ether; space; sky; literally: "not visible." The subtlest of the five elements (panchabhuta), from which the other four arise. It is all-pervading, and is sometimes identified with consciousness–chidakasha. It is the basis of sound (shabda), which is its particular property.

Akashavani: Ethereal voice; heavenly voice.

Akasha Tattwa: The ether-principle.

Akhanda: Unbroken (literally: "not broken"); indivisible; undivided; whole.

Aklishta: Unafflicted; non-afflicted; unmoved.

Akshara: Imperishable; indestructible, immutable, undying; undecaying; unchanging–all in reference to the individual self and the Supreme Self, Brahman.

Akula: Without form; formless.

Alabdhabhumikatva: Non-achievement of a stage; inability to find a footing.

Alambana: Support.

Alakshana: Without distinctive marks.

Alasya: Laziness; idleness; apathy; sloth.

Alata chakra: A stick burning at one end, when waved round quickly, produces an illusion of a circle of fire.

Alinga: Without any attribute, characteristic or mark; Parabrahman; noumenal; undifferentiated prakriti.

Amala: Without impurity.

Amalaka: Embelica myrobalan

Amalam: Free from Maya; free from the impurity of Maya.

Amana/Amanaska: Mindless.

Amangala: Inauspicious.

Amanitwam: Humility; absence of pride.

Amara: Immortal; deathless.

Amatam: Unperceivable.

Amatra: Having no sign.

Amavasya: New moon day.

Ambara: Sky ; ether; cloth; garment.

Amrita: That which makes one immortal. The nectar of immortality that emerged from the ocean of milk when the gods churned it.

Amsha: Part; component; limb; fragment.

Anadi: Beginningless; eternal.

Anahata: "Unstruck;" "unbeaten." Continuous bell-like inner resonance; the heart; the heart chakra; the inner divine melody (mystic sounds heard by the Yogis); supernatural sound; So'ham.

Anahata chakra: "Unstruck." Energy center located in the spine at the point opposite the center of the chest (sternum bone). Seat of the Air element.

Anahata-dhvani: Mystic sounds heard by Yogis.

Ananda: Bliss; happiness; joy. A fundamental attribute of Brahman, which is Satchidananda: Existence, Consciousness, Bliss.

Ananda sagara: Ocean of Bliss.

Anandamaya: Full of bliss.

Anandamaya kosha: "The sheath of bliss (ananda)." The causal body (karana sharira). The borderline of the Self (atman).

Anandamayi Ma: One of the major spiritual figures in twentieth-century India, first made known to the West by Paramhansa Yogananda in his *Autobiography of a Yogi*.

Ananta: Infinite; without end; endless; a name of Shesha, the chief of the Nagas, whose coils encircle the earth and who symbolizes eternity, and upon whom Vishnu reclines.

Anarabdha-karya: Works which have not yet begun to produce their effects.

Anarya(n): Not aryan; ignoble; unworthy. See Aryan.

Anatma(n): Not-Self; insentient.

Anavashtitatvani: Unsteadiness; instability of mind; inability to find a footing; mental unsteadiness.

Aneka: Not one–i.e., many.

Anga: Limb; individual part; accessory; member; step d. The yoga expounded by Pantanjali in the Yoga Sutras (Yoga Darshan) has eight limbs: yama, niyama, asana, pranayama, dharana, dhyana, pratyahara, and samadhi.

Angamejayatva: Shaking of the body; lack of control over the body.

Anima: Subtlety; the power of making the body subtle; reducing the physical mass and density at will; one of the eight Siddhis.

Anishta: Undesired; bad.

Anitya: Impermanent; transient.

Anna: In the old currency, there were sixteen annas in a rupee. In the modern currency, twenty-five and fifty pice coins are called four and eight annas, respectively, but it is not really so.

Anna(m): Food; matter. In the old currency, there were sixteen annas in a rupee. In the modern currency, twenty-five and fifty pice coins are called four and eight annas, respectively, but it is not really so.

Annamaya kosha: "The sheath of food (anna)." The physical–or gross–body, made of food.

Annapurna: "Full of Food." A title of the Goddess (Shakti) depicted as the Goddess of Food and Abundance. The consort of Shiva.

Anrita: Falsehood or untruth.

Anta: End.

Antahkarana: Internal instrument; the subtle bodies; fourfold mind: mind, intellect, ego and subconscious mind.

Antahkarana-chatushtaya: The mind in its four aspects, viz., Manas, Buddhi, Citta and Ahamkara; fourfold internal organ.

Antah-prajna: Inner subjective consciousness.

Antar: Internal; middle; interspace.

Antaranga: Internal organ; mind.

Antaratma(n): Inner Self; conscience.

Antardrishti: Inner vision.

Antarika: Inward; whole-hearted.

Antariksha: Firmament; sky.

Antarmukha: Literally "inner face"–inward vision or perception.

Antarmukha vritti: A state in which the mind is turned inwards and is withdrawn from objects.

Antaryamana: Ruling within.

Antaryamin: Indweller; inner guide; inner ruler; God as the Inner Controller.

Anu: Atom; of minute size.

Anubhava: Perception; direct personal experience; identity of the Jiva with Brahman; spiritual experience; intuitive consciousness and knowledge.

Anubhava-advaita: Actual living experience of Oneness.

Anugraha: Divine grace; attraction; favor; kindness, conferring benefits; assistance.

Anukarah: Following; imitating.

Anumana: Inference.

Anumanika: Inferential.

Anuswara: Bindu.

Anusandhana: Enquiry or investigation; in Vedanta, enquiry or investigation into the nature of Brahman.

Anuraga: Intense prema or love (towards God).

Anushaya: The balance or residue of karma which forces the soul to take rebirth in this or the other world after temporary freedom enjoyed in the higher spheres.

Anushthana: Observance; religious exercise; repetition of a mantra for a set number of times during a given period; systematic performance of religious practices, usually undertaken for some definite period of time.

Anusmarana: Remembrance; constant memory of Brahman or God.

Anvaya-vyatireka: Positive and negative assertions; proof by assertion and negation. Just as several kinds of dal are mixed together, so also, the Atman is mixed with the five koshas. You will have to separate the Self from the five sheaths. You will have to separate name and form from Existence-Knowledge-Bliss Absolute. Anvaya and vyatireka processes always go together. The Self exists in the five sheaths, yet it is not the sheaths. This is Vedantic sadhana. The aspirant rejects the names and forms and the five sheaths and realizes the one, all-pervading, indivisible, infinite, eternal, unchanging essence, viz., Brahman.

Apah: Water.

Apamana: Disrespect; disgrace.

Apana: The prana that moves downward, producing the excretory functions in general; exhalation.

Apara: Lower; lower knowledge; other; relative; inferior.

Aparadha: Fault; mistake.

Aparajita: Unconquerable.

Aparigraha: Non-possessiveness, non-greed, non-selfishness, non-acquisitiveness; freedom from covetousness; non-receiving of gifts conducive to luxury.

Aparna: Imperfect; not full; incomplete.

Aparoksha: Direct; immediate.

Aparoksha anubhuti: The direct, immediate, intuitive experience or perception of the invisible—the realization of Brahman. The title of a treatise on Advaita Vedanta by Shankaracharya.

Aparokshanubhava-svarupa: The essence of direct intuitive perception; of the nature or form of direct realization.

Aparokshatva: Feeling of directness or immediateness.

Apavarga: Liberation; release; escape from pain; release from the bondage of embodiment.

Apavitra: Impure.

Aprajnata: Unknown

Apsara: A celestial damsel, nymph, and dancer.

Apta: Competent person; a sage or an adept; a wellwisher.

Apunya: Demerit; vice; non-meritorious acts; unvirtuous deeds; sinful. See Punya.

Aradhana: Worship of the Divine; adoration; self-surrender.

Arambha: Origin; cause; original; causal. Mental initiation of an action; sankalpa.

Arambha-vada: "The theory of origination;" the doctrine of the creation of the world by Ishwara; the theory of a beginning, an origination, a creation of the world by an agency external to the questioner; the doctrine of an absolute new creation; the theory of the Nyaya Vaisesika.

Arani: Sacrificial wood stick for creating fire through friction.

Aranya: Forest.

Aranyaka: "Forest book;" philosophical, symbolic, and spiritual interpretations of the Vedic hymns and rituals. Mainly meant for forest-dwelling ascetics (vanaprasthas).

Arati: A ceremony of worship in which lights, incense, camphor, and other offerings representing the five elements and the five senses–the totality of the human being–are waved before an image or symbol of the Divine.

Aratrika: See Arati.

Archa(nam): Worship; adoration; offering of flowers and sacred leaves, etc., at the time of puja or worship, uttering the names of the object of worship.

Ardhangini: Partner in life (wife); especially Parvati, the wife of Lord Siva.

Arghya: Offering of water made in ritualistic worship. Sometimes an offering of flowers, bel leaves, sandal paste, durva grass, and rice together.

Arjava(m): Straightforwardness; simplicity; honesty; rectitude of conduct (from the verb root *rinj*: "to make straight"); uprightness.

Arjuna: The great disciple of Krishna, who imparted to him the teachings found in the Bhagavad Gita. The third of the Pandava brothers who were major figures in the Mahabharata War. His name literally means "bright," "white," or "clear."

Arta(m): Pain(ed); distress(ed); affliction (afflicted); one who is seeking/asking for relief from personal troubles or suffering.

Artha: Wealth; object; thing; meaning; sense; purpose; an object of desire. It is the secular value which is both desired and desirable. It satisfies the acquisitive tendency in individuals. It is the economic value.

Arya(n): One who is an Arya–literally, "one who strives upward." Both Arya and Aryan are exclusively psychological terms having nothing whatsoever to do with birth, race, or nationality. In his teachings Buddha habitually referred to spiritually qualified people as "the Aryas." Although in English translations we find the expressions: "The Four Noble Truths," and "The Noble Eightfold Path," Buddha actually said: "The Four Aryan Truths," and "The Eightfold Aryan Path."

Arya Dharma: The Dharma of the Aryas. See Sanatana Dharma.

Arya Samaj: The organization founded by Maharshi Dayananda Saraswati in the nineteenth century to encourage the restoration of the more ancient and simple forms of original Vedic religion.

Aryaman: Chief of the Pitris.

Aryavarta: The land of the Aryas. Usually applied to northern India.

Asambhava: Total inapplicability; impossibility.

Asamprajñata samadhi: Highest superconscious state where the mind and the ego-sense are completely annihilated. Superconscious union; a stage in samadhi wherein one is not conscious of any object and in the mind ceases to function.

Asamprayoga: Withdrawal of the senses from their objects; non-communication; non-interchange; withdrawal; disuniting; disconnecting.

Asana: Posture; seat; meditation posture; Hatha Yoga posture.

Asanga: Non-attachment; without attachment.

Asara: Without essence; dry; barren; worthless.

Asat: Unreal[ity]; nonbeing; nonexistence; false; falsehood.

Asatya: Unreal; untrue.

Asha: Hope; expectation.

Ashanaya: Desire to eat or consume; hunger.

Ashanayapipashe: Hunger and thirst

Ashanti: Absence of peace of mind; restlessness; distraction.

Ashaucha: Impurity; uncleanness.

Ashishah: Primordial will; drive-to-survive; will-to-live; desire to live; expectation. From *a* which means near to or toward, and *shas* which means to order or direct. It is the force within the individual that causes it to pass from the absolute into the conditioned, from the transcendent into the immanent condition, from eternity into time, into relative existence.

Ashram(a): A place for spiritual discipline and study, usually a monastic residence. Also a stage of life. In Hinduism life is divided ideally into four stages (ashramas): 1) the celibate student life (brahmacharya); 2) the married household life (grihasta); 3) the life of retirement (seclusion) and contemplation (vanaprastha); 4) the life of total renunciation (sannyasa).

Ashrama-dharma: Duties pertaining to the four order or stages of life.

Ashramite: Resident of an ashram.

Ashrutam: Unhearable.

Ashtami: "The eighth"–eighth day of the dark or light fortnights of the lunar cycle.

Ashtanga Yoga: The "eight-limbed" Yoga of Patanjali consisting of yama, niyama, asana, pranayama, pratyahara, dharana, dhyana, and samadhi (see separate entries for each "limb").

Ashuchi: Impure; not clean.

Ashuddha: Impure; incorrect.

Ashuddhi: Impurity.

Ashwattha: The pippal (sacred fig) tree, in the Bhagavad Gita, the eternal tree of life whose roots are in heaven. The "world tree" in the sense of the axis of the earth and even of the cosmos.

Ashwins: Two Vedic deities, celestial horsemen of the sun, always together, who herald the dawn and are skilled in healing. They avert misfortune and sickness and bring treasures.

Ashubha: Inauspicious, unfortunate.

Asmi: I am; I exist.

Asmita: I-ness; the sense of "I am;" "I exist;" sense of individuality.

Asteya: Non-stealing; honesty; non-misappropriativeness.

Asthira: Wavering and unsteady.

Asti: Exists; is; Brahman.

Astikyam: Piety; belief in God.

Astra: Missile; weapon invoked with a Mantra.

Asura: Demon; evil being (a-sura: without the light).

Asuric: Of demonic character.

Asurim: The state of an asura, one who dwells in darkness (a-sura—without the light). The condition of those negative souls who are turned away from divinity and moving further into degradation of consciousness and mode of life.

Asurisampat: Devilish qualities; demonaical wealth.

Aswara: Without sound, accent, or tone.

Atattwa: The absolute opposite of Tattwa; non-principle; non-element; non-essence; untruth; unreality.

Atiprashna: Transcendental question; too much questioning; questioning carried to the extreme.

Atita: Past; above; beyond; transcendent.

Atma(n): The individual spirit or Self that is one with Brahman. The true nature or identity.

Atmabala: Soul-force.

Atma-bhava: The nature of the Self; awareness of the self; feeling: "I am the Self."

Atma-bodha: Knowledge of the Self; also a work of that name by Sri Sankara.

Atma-cintana: Reflection on the Self or the Atman.

Atma-darshan: The seeing or sight of the Self (atma); the vision of the Self; knowledge of the Self through direct vision or knowing; the vision of seeing everything as the Self.

Atma-drishti: Atma-darshan.

Atma shakti: Power of the Self; personal power or strength.

Atmajna: One who has known the Self; seer with Self-knowledge.

Atmajnana: Direct knowledge of the Self; Brahma-Jnana.

Atmajnani: One who has atmajnana.

Atmalakshya: Having the Self as the goal; Self as the object of meditation of Vedantins.

Atmanistha: Established in the Self.

Atmanivedana: Dedicating one's entire self to the divine; self-surrender.

Atmaprabha: Light of the Self; shining by one's own light; self-illuminated or Self-illuminated: illuminated by one's own true Self. Light of the Self; shining by one's own light; self-illuminated or Self-illuminated: illuminated by one's own true Self.

Atmaprakasha: The shining forth or light of the Self.

Atmapratyaksha: Direct perception of the Self.

Atmarama: Satisfied–delighted–in the Self.

Atmarati: Rejoicing in the Self; interested or centred in the Self.

Atmasakshatkara: "Direct sight of the Self;" realization of the true nature of the Self; Self-realization.

Atmasamarpana: Self-consecration; offering of the self, at the feet of the Lord.

Atmatripti: Satisfaction in one's own Self.

Atmavichara: Enquiry into the Self.

Atmavidya: Teaching about the Self and its reality; knowledge of the Self.

Atmavit: Knower of the Self.

Atmic: Having to do with the atma–spirit or self.

Atyantabhava: Complete non-existence; extreme unreality, like the horn of a rabbit or a lotus in the sky or the son of a barren woman.

Aum: Alternate spelling of Om.

Aurobindo Ghosh, Sri: One of India's greatest yogis and spiritual writers, he was at first involved in the Indian freedom movement, but came to see that yoga was the true path to freedom. His ashram in South India became one of the major spiritual centers in modern India, and his voluminous spiritual writings are read and prized throughout the world.

Aushadi: Herb; medicine.

Avadhuta: "Cast off" (one who has cast off the world utterly). A supreme ascetic and jnani who has renounced all worldly attachments and connections and lives in a state beyond body consciousness, whose behavior is not bound by ordinary social conventions. Usually they wear no clothing. They embody the highest state of asceticism or tapas.

Avarana: Concealment; veil; screen; obstruction; the veiling power of ignorance.

Avarana-shakti: Veiling power of Maya; Avidya in

the individual.

Avastha: State of experience; state of consciousness; condition.

Avastu: Non-material; non-substance; nothing; without the characteristic of a thing as being spacebound and time-tied; unsubstantial.

Avatar(a): A fully liberated spirit (jiva) who is born into a world below Satya Loka to help others attain liberation. Though commonly referred to as a divine incarnation, an avatar actually is totally one with God, and therefore an incarnation of God-Consciousness.

Avidya: Ignorance; nescience; unknowing; literally: "to know not." A Sakti or illusive power in Brahman which is sometimes regarded as one with Maya and sometimes as different from it. It forms the condition of the individual soul and is otherwise called Ajnana or Asuddha-maya. It forms the Karana Sarira of the Jiva. It is Malina or impure Sattwa. Also called ajnana.

Avidyamaya: Maya, or illusion causing duality, has two aspects, namely, avidyamaya and vidyamaya. Avidyamaya, or the "maya of ignorance," consisting of anger, passion, and so on, entangles one in worldliness. Vidyamaya, or the "maya of knowledge," consisting of kindness, purity, unselfishness, and so on, leads one to liberation. Both belong to the relative world. See Maya.

Avidyasakti: The power of ignorance (avidya).

Avijnatam: Unknowable

Avinashi: Indestructible; imperishable.

Avirati: Hankering after objects; non-dispassion; sensual indulgence; lack of control; non-restraint.

Avritta-cakshuh: One whose gaze is turned inwards.

Avyakrita: Undifferentiated; undefined; unexpounded; inconceivable; unanswerable questions; the elementary substance from which all things were created, considered as one with the substance of Brahman.

Avyakta(m): Unmanifest; invisible; when the three gunas are in a state of equilibrium' the undifferentiated.

Avyakta-nada: Unmanifested sound.

Avyaya: Inexhaustible; undiminishing; unchangeable

Ayam Atma Brahma: "This Self is Brahman." The Mahavakya (Great Saying) of the Mandukya Upanishad).

Ayana: Movement; the sun's passage northward and southward from the tropics of cancer and capricorn.

Ayurveda: "Life-knowledge." The ancient system of Indian medicine formulated by the sage Dhanvantari and considered part of the Vedic revelation.

B

Baba: A title often given to sadhus, saints and yogis, meaning "father." Little children are sometimes affectionately called "baba" by adults.

Baddha: Bound; one who is in a state of bondage.

Bahusyam: "May I be many" the original "thought" or sankalpa of Brahman before the projection of creation.

Bahya: External; outward.

Bal(a)krishna: The child/boy Krishna.

Bala brahmacharya: Brahmacharya observed from childhood (bala).

Balarama: Sri Krishna's elder brother, also called "Balai."

Bandha: "Lock;" bond; bondage; tie or knot; a Hatha Yoga exercise.

Bel: A tree whose leaves are sacred to Siva; also the fruit of the same tree.

Bhadra: Blessing; happy; well.

Bhagavad Gita: "The Song of God." The sacred philosophical text often called "the Hindu Bible," part of the epic Mahabharata by Vyasa; the most popular sacred text in Hinduism.

Bhagavan: The Lord; the One endowed with the six attributes, viz. infinite treasures, strength, glory, splendor knowledge, and renunciation; the Personal God.

Bhagavata: A devotee of God (Bhagavan) or Vishnu.

Bhagavatam: Srimad Bhagavatam. A major purana devoted to the glory and worship of Vishnu and his incarnation as Krishna. The major scripture of the Vaishnavas.

Bhagavati: Goddess; the feminine form of Bhagavan.

Bhairava: Shiva.

Bhairavi: A nun of the Tantric sect.

Bhajan: Devotional singing; a devotional song; remembrance (of God).

Bhajana: Worship (of the Lord); praise (of the Lord); taking refuge (in the Lord).

Bhakta: Devotee; votary; a follower of the path of bhakti, divine love; a worshipper of the Personal God.

Bhakti: Devotion; dedication; love (of God).

Bhakti Marga: The path of devotion leading to union with God.

Bhakti Sutra: An aphoristic work on devotional Yoga authored by the sage Narada. Another text by the same title is ascribed to the sage Shandilya.

Bhakti Yoga: The yoga of attaining union with God through the prescribed spiritual discipline of the path of devotion.

Bhakti Yogi: One who practices Bhakti Yoga.

Bhaktivedanta (Swami): The founder of the Hari Krishna movement in America.

Bharat(a): The proper Sanskrit name for India; one of the brothers of Rama; a title of Arjuna.

Bharati: Indian

Bharat(a)varsha: The land of India.

Bhashya: Commentary.

Bhautika: Pertaining to or composed of elements; material; physical.

Bhati: Shining; self-luminous; light; splendor; intelligence, consciousness.

Bhava: Subjective state of being (existence); attitude of mind; mental attitude or feeling; state of realization in the heart or mind.

Bhava samadhi: Superconscious state attained by bhaktas or devotees through intense divine emotion in which the devotee retains his ego and enjoys communion with the Personal God.

Bhavamukha: An exalted state of spiritual experience, in which the aspirant keeps his mind on the borderline between the Absolute and the Relative. From this position he can contemplate the ineffable and attributeless Brahman and also participate in the activities of the relative world, seeing in it the manifestation of God alone.

Bhavanam: Meditation. "Bhavanam is setting the heart on the Lord" (Shankara, Commentary on the Yoga Sutras). It has the connotation of all the awareness becoming focused and absorbed in it.

Bhavatarini: "Savior of the World (or Universe);" a title of the Divine Mother, especially Kali.

Bhaya: Fear; terror.

Bheda: Difference distinction; disjunction; splitting.

Bhedabheda: Difference and non-difference; a system of philosophy in which the individual is different from and one with the Supreme Soul.

Bhedabuddhi: The intellect that creates differences: the vyavaharika buddhi that diversifies everything as opposed to the paramartic buddhi that unifies everything.

Bhiksha: Almsfood; food obtained by begging or that is offered to a monk.

Bhikshu: One who lives on bhiksha (almsfood); a mendicant; a sannyasi; also a designation of a Buddhist monk.

Bhoga: Enjoyment, pleasure; experience; perception; also food (usually what has been offered to a deity).

Bhogya: Object of experience or enjoyment.

Bhokta: Enjoyer; experiencer; subject of experience or enjoyment.

Bhrama: Illusion; delusion; rotation; wandering.

Bhranti: Delusion; wrong notion; false idea or impression.

Bhrashta: Fallen from the way of Yoga.

Bhrigu: An ancient sage, so illustrious that he mediated quarrels among the gods.

Bhrikuti: Space between the eye-brows.

Bhuh: The earth-plane.

Bhukti: Material enjoyment.

Bhuma: The unconditioned Infinite; Brahman.

Bhumi: The earth; ground; region; place.

Bhuta (1): What has come into being; an entity as opposed to the unmanifested; any of the five elementary constituents of the universe; element.

Bhuta (2): A spirit. Some bhutas are subhuman nature spirits or "elementals," but some are earthbound human spirits—ghosts. Bhutas may be either positive or negative.

Bhuvah: The higher etheric or the astral world.

Bhuvana: World.

Bija: Seed; source.

Bija Mantra: A "seed" mantra from which realization grows as a tree from a seed; usually a single-syllable mantra.

Bijakshara: The root-letter or the seed-letter in which there is the latent power of a Mantra.

Bijatma: The subtle inner Self; also called Sukshmatma, Sutratma or Antaryamin.

Bimba: Original; (Brahman).

Bimbapratibimbavada: The doctrine that the Jiva is a reflection of Brahman; Jiva who is the reflection of Brahman is not, therefore, a distinct thing from but is absolutely one with It. This is one phase of the theory of reflection which lays stress on the identity of the reflection and the original.

Bindu: Point; dot; seed; source; the creative potency of anything where all energies are focused; the point from which the subtle Omkara arises that is experienced in meditation.

Bodha: Consciousness; intelligence; wisdom; knowledge; "to be awake;" enlightenment.

Bodhi: Enlightenment; "to be awakened;" the state of the awakened yogi, or buddha.

Brahma: The Creator (Prajapati) of the three worlds of men, angels, and archangels (Bhur, Bhuwah, and Swah); the first of the created beings; Hiranyagarbha or cosmic intelligence.

Brahma satyam; jagan mithya; jivo brahmaiva naparah: "Brahman is real. The world is illusion. The jiva is none other than Brahman." This is Shankara's renowned "Vedanta in half a verse."

Brahma Sutras: A treatise by Vyasa on Vedanta philosophy in the form of aphorisms. Also called the Vedanta Sutras or Vedanta Darshana.

Brahma-anubhava: Direct personal experience of Brahman.

Brahmabhata: One who has become Brahman.

Brahmabhava(na): Feeling of identity with Brahman, as well as of everything as Brahman.

Brahmabhavanam: Meditation on Brahman; feeling of identity with Brahman, as well as of everything as Brahman.

Brahmabhyasa: Meditation on Brahman; Nididhydsana; reflection on Brahman; conversing on Brahman; discussing about Brahman; etc., that is calculated to the realization of Brahman.

Brahmachaitanya: Divine Consciousness, Brahman-Consciousness.

Brahmachari(n): One who observes continence; a celibate student in the first stage of life (ashrama); a junior monk.

Brahmacharini: Female "brahmachari."

Brahmacharya: Continence; self-restraint on all levels; discipline; dwelling in Brahman.

Brahmacharya-ashrama: Order of the students engaged in the study of the Vedas and the service of the Guru or the preceptor.

Brahmachintana: Constant meditation on Brahman; constant thought of or awareness of God.

Brahmajnana: Direct, transcendental knowledge of Brahman; Self-realization.

Brahmajnani: One who possess Brahmajnana.

Brahmajyoti: The Light of God.

Brahmakaravritti: The sole ultimate thought of Brahman alone to the exclusion of all other thoughts that is arrived at through intense Vedantic meditation.

Brahmaloka: The world (loka) of God (Brahman); the infinite consciousness of God.

Brahmamaya: Formed of Brahma; filled with Brahma.

Brahmamuhurta: "The muhurta of Brahman." The period of one and a half hours before sunrise (sometime between 3:00 a.m. and 6:00 a.m.), which is said to be the best time for meditation and worship.

Brahman: The Absolute Reality; the Truth proclaimed in the Upanishads; the Supreme Reality that is one and indivisible, infinite, and eternal; all-pervading, changeless Existence; Existence-knowledge-bliss Absolute (Satchidananda); Absolute Consciousness; it is not only all-powerful but all-power itself; not only all-knowing and blissful but all-knowledge and all-bliss itself.

Brahmana (1): A knower of Brahman; a Brahmajnani.

Brahmana (2): A member of the Brahmin caste.

Brahmana (3): A Vedic liturgical text explaining the rituals found in the Vedic samhitas (collection of hymns). A guidebook for performing those rites.

Brahmananda: The bliss of communion with Brahman.

Brahmanda: "The egg of Brahma" or "the Brahmic egg." The cosmic "egg;" the universe; the cosmos; the macrocosm.

Brahmanirvana: The state of liberation (nirvana) that results from total union with Brahman.

Brahmanishtha: Remaining steadfast in the Absolute (Brahman). One who is firmly established in the Supreme being, in the direct knowledge of Brahman, the Absolute Reality.

Brahmanubhava: Self-realization; God-realization; absolute experience.

Brahmanusandhana: Considering, thinking of, searching after, enquiring into, looking after, investigation of, exploration into the nature of Brahman; receiving of the Upadesha about Brahman and reflection upon it.

Brahma-parayana: One whose faith and sole refuge is in Brahman.

Brahmarandhra: "The hole of Brahman," the subtle (astral) aperture in the crown of the head. Said to be the gateway to the Absolute (Brahman) in the thousand-petaled lotus (sahasrara) in the crown of the head. Liberated beings are said to exit the physical body through this aperture at death.

Brahmarishi: A knower of Brahman.

Brahmasakshatkara: Realization of Brahman; direct experience of the Absolute Being.

Brahmashakti: The power of the Supreme Being.

Brahmasamstha: Grounded in Brahman; Sannyasin.

Brahmastithi (or Brahmistithi): The establishment or

dwelling in Brahman.

Brahmatejas: The effulgent splendor of Brahman.

Brahmavada: The Path to Brahman; the way to supreme enlightenment.

Brahmavadin: Literally "one who walks the path of Brahman." One who advocates that there is one existence alone–Parabrahman.

Brahmavakya: Divine revelation, such as the Upanishads.

Brahmavichara: Enquiry into the Absolute (Brahman).

Brahmavidya: Science of Brahman; knowledge of Brahman; learning pertaining to Brahman or the Absolute Reality.

Brahmavit: Knower of Brahman.

Brahmayoga: State in which the Yogi realizes himself and the whole universe as Brahman.

Brihat: Large; big; absolute.

Brahmic: Divine; pertaining to God (Brahman).

Brahmin (Brahmana): A knower of Brahman; a member of the highest Hindu caste traditionally consisting of priests, pandits, philosophers, and religious leaders.

Brahmopasana: Worship of the Infinite Brahman.

Bhranti-darshana: Delusion; erroneous view.

Brihaspati: The guru–priest and teacher–of the gods.

Brihatsaman: A hymn to Indra found in the Sama Veda.

Brindaban: The place where Krishna was born and where he lived until the age of twelve. Today it is a city of devotees and temples. Many agree with my friend who once said to me in a very matter-of-fact way: "Brindaban is my life." Its actual name is Vrindavan, but so many Bengali devotees and saints for centuries have called it "Brindaban" in their dialect, it has become common usage throughout India.

Buddha: "An awakened one;" one full of knowledge who has attained enlightenment (bodhi), and thereby moksha (liberation). The usual reference to Gautama (Sakyamuni) Buddha of the sixth century B.C,

Buddhi: Intellect; intelligence; understanding; reason; the thinking mind; the higher mind, which is the seat of wisdom; the discriminating faculty.

Buddhi-sattwa: Experience of the buddhi in its most subtle level in which the buddhi and the Self are virtually indistinguishable; the experience of I-am (asmita/aham), experience of the Self through the buddhi.

Buddhi-shakti: Intellectual power.

Buddhi-shuddhi: Purity of intellect.

Buddhi-tattwa: Principle of intelligence.

Buddhi Yoga: The Yoga of Intelligence spoken of in the Bhagavad Gita which later came to be called Jnana Yoga, the Yoga of Knowledge.

C

Caste: See Varna.

Chaitanya: Consciousness; intelligence; awareness; the consciousness that knows itself and knows others; Pure Consciousness.

Chaitanyamayi: Full of (all-) consciousness; an attribute of Maya.

Chaitanya-samadhi: The state of superconsciousness which is marked by absolute self-awareness and illumination as distinguished from Jada-samadhi in which there is no such awareness.

Chakra: Wheel. Plexus; center of psychic energy in the human system, particularly in the spine or head.

Chakshuh: Eye; the visual sense or faculty; the subtle organ of sight; sense of seeing.

Chamatkara: Remarkable traits and abilities; cleverness; shining forth with divine glory.

Chandala: An untouchable, or outcaste; literally: "wild" or "bad."

Chandra: Presiding deity of the moon or the astral lunar world (loka).

Chandranadi: The lunar psychic current that flows through the left nostril.

Charana: Foot; one-fourth; conduct.

Charanamrita: Water sanctified by bathing the feet of a deity or of a holy man with it.

Charu: A preparation of boiled rice, milk, sugar and ghee, to be offered into the fire for gods; a sattvic dietary regimen usually taken by yoga-practitioners and celibates. Havishya.

Charvaka: The Indian materialistic school, also known as Lokayata ("restricted to the world of common experience"). Its central teaching is that matter is the only reality, and sense perception is the only valid means of knowledge or proof. Therefore sense satisfaction is the only goal.

Chaturvarga: Fourfold aims, viz., dharma, artha, kama, and moksha.

Chaturyuga: The four ages of the Hindu world-cycle, viz., krta treta dvapara, and kali.

Chela: Disciple.

Cheshta: Endeavor; effort; activity.

Chetana: Consciousness. Whereas chaitanya is the principle of pure consciousness, chetana is consciousness occupied with an object. It is this "consciousness" that Buddha rejected as an obstacle.

Chetas: Subconscious mind.

Chidabhasa: Reflected consciousness; the reflection of intelligence which resides in the internal organ (anthakarana).

Chidakasha: "The Space (Ether) of Consciousness." The

infinite, all-pervading expanse of Consciousness from which all "things" proceed; the subtle space of Consciousness in the Sahasrara (Thousand-petalled Lotus). The true "heart" of all things. Brahman in Its aspect as limitless knowledge; unbounded intelligence. This is a familiar concept of the Upanishads. It is not meant that the physical ether is consciousness. The Pure Consciousness (Cit) is like the ether (Akasa), an all-pervading continuum.

Chidananda: Consciousness-Bliss.

Chinmaya: Full of consciousness; formed of consciousness.

Chinta: Sorrow; worry.

Chintana: Thinking; reflecting.

Chit: Consciousness (that is spirit or purusha); "to perceive, observe, think, be aware, know;" pure unitary Consciousness. The principle of universal intelligence or consciousness.

Chitraratha: The chief of the gandharvas.

Chitshakti: Power of consciousness or intelligence.

Chitswarupa: Of the very form of pure intelligence or consciousness.

Chitta: The subtle energy that is the substance of the mind, and therefore the mind itself; mind in all its aspects; the field of the mind; the field of consciousness; consciousness itself; the subconscious mind.

Chittakasha: Mental ether; mind conceived of as ether (all-pervading).

Chitta-shuddhi: Purity or clarity or the chitta; purification or clarification of the chitta.

Chittavidya: Psychology; science of the mind and the sub-conscience.
Chittavimukti: Freedom from the bondage of the mind
Chitta-vritti-nirodha: Cessation of the modifications of the mind; control of thoughts; Patanjali's definition of Yoga.
Collyrium (Khol): A black substance put around the eyes. Though used cosmetically, it is considered to have medicinal properties that protect the eyes from infection or disease. It is often put around children's eyes for this purpose.
Crore: Ten million.

D

Dacoit: A violent thief who preys on travelers, sometimes killing them.
Dada: Uncle.
Dahara: Dwelling-place; abode.
Daityas: Demons who constantly war with the gods. Sometimes "races" or nationalities who acted contrary to dharma and fought against the "aryas" were also called demons (daityas or asuras); giant; titan.
Daiva: God Who controls all beings and gives them what is their due; belonging to or coming from the gods/God; celestial; divine; fate; destiny; controlling power.
Daivi: Same as Divya; divine.
Daivim: The state of a deva or "shining one;" the quality of those positive souls who are progressing toward divinity.
Daksha: Expert; intelligent; wise; able.
Dakshina: Gift; priestly gift; sacrificial fee; donation; an offering given as a gift of gratitude; guru dakshina is that given at the time of initiation.
Dakshinamurti: A name for Lord Shiva as the silent teacher.

Vedic Religion declares that in every cycle of creation God manifests as Dakshinamurti and becomes the guru of the first human beings–those who were most spiritually evolved in the previous creation–teaching them the path to liberation (moksha).

Dakshineshwar: A village on the Ganges about five miles north of Calcutta, where, in the 1850's, the Rani Rasmani built a compound of temples: the Kali temple, twelve small Shiva temples, and the Radhakanta (Radha-Krishna) temple. Just north of the northernmost Shiva temple is the room which Sri Ramakrishna occupied for a considerable part of his life.

Dakshyam: Skill; virtuosity; dexterity.

Dama: Self-control; control of the senses; restraint.

Damaru: A small, handheld drum with two heads that is sounded by twisting the wrist and causing a ball tied to its middle to rhythmically strike the heads alternately.

Dambha: Hypocrisy; pride.

Dana: "Giving;" gift; charity; almsgiving; self-sacrifice; donation; generosity.

Danda: The staff of a mendicant or a Sanyasin; a kind of physical exercise common in India; punishment.

Darbha: A kind of grass held sacred for religious and spiritual purposes.

Darpa: Arrogance; pride.

Darshan: Literally "sight" or "seeing;" vision, literal and metaphysical; a system of philosophy (see Sad-darshanas). Darshan is the seeing of a holy being as well as the blessing received by seeing such a one.

Darshana: "Seeing" in the sense of a viewpoint or system of thought. The Sad-darshanas are the six orthodox systems of Indian philosophy: Nyaya, Vaisheshika, Sankhya, Yoga, Mimamsa, and Vedanta.

Dasa: Slave; servant.

Dasanami: "Ten named." A term for members of the monastic order of Shankaracharya headquartered in the four quarters of India (Sringeri, Dwaraka, Badrinath and Jagannath Puri). After their proper monastic names they add one of ten titles (Saraswati, Bharati, Puri, Tirtha, Ashrama, Giri, Parvata, Sagara, Vanam, Aranya) according to their monastic succession.

Dasya: The attitude of a devotee expressing the relationship of a servant with God.

Dasyu: A slave; a symbolic term used in the Vedas for those of low and bound consciousness who are the opposite of the Aryans.

Datta: Given; adopted; give.

Dattatreya: A famous sage, son of the Rishi Atri and Anasuya. His birth was a divine boon, hence his name: Datta–"given"–and atreya–"son of Atri." Considered a divine incarnation and known as the Lord of Avadhutas, he is often revered as the embodiment of the Supreme Guru. He is credited with the authorship of the *Avadhuta* Gita, the *Jivanmukti Gita*, and the *Tripura Rahashya*.

Daurmanasya: Despair, depression etc., caused by mental sickness; feeling of wretchedness and miserableness.

Daya: Mercy; compassion; grace; empathy.

Dayananda (Maharishi Swami): A leading reformer within Hinduism in the nineteenth century (1824-1883) and the founder of the Arya Samaj.

Deha: Physical body.

Dehabhimana: Egoistic attachment to the body.

Dehadhyasa: False identification with the body.

Dehashuddhi: Purity or purification of the body.

Dehi: One who has a body; the conscious embodied self; Jiva or the individual soul.

Desha: Place; locus; spot; space; country.

Deva: "A shining one," a god–greater or lesser in the evolutionary hierarchy; a semi-divine or celestial being with great powers, and therefore a "god." Sometimes called a demi-god. Devas are the demigods presiding over various powers of material and psychic nature. In many instances "devas" refer to the powers of the senses or the sense organs themselves.

Devaloka: The world (loka) of the gods.

Devata: Godhead; god; divinity; celestial being. See Deva.

Devatma: The divine, inner Self.

Devayana: The way or path of the gods, "the shining ones;" the path that leads beyond earthly rebirth and ultimately to liberation.

Devi: Goddess; the Supreme Shakti (Divine Power) or Divine Mother, or a demigoddess.

Dhairya: Boldness; courage.

Dhana: Wealth; riches.

Dhanvantari: The great rishi who first revealed the principles of Ayurveda to his students.

Dhara: Stream; continuous repetition.

Dharana: Concentration of mind; fixing the mind upon a single thing or point. "Dharana is the confining [fixing] of the mind within a point or area" (Yoga Sutras 3:1).

Dharma (1): The righteous way of living, as enjoined by the sacred scriptures and the spiritually illumined; law; lawfulness; virtue; righteousness; norm.

Dharma (2): Attributes; natures; essential/visible characteristics; characteristic form; properties; qualifications.

Dharma-megha samadhi: The final state of one-pointedness, when an individual becomes disinterested even in omniscience, omnipotence, and omnipresence. This state of superconsciousness or samadhi is called dharma-megha–cloud of virtue–inasmuch as it showers nectar drops of immortality through knowledge of Brahman, when all the hosts of vasanas are entirely destroyed. This state of superconsciousness or Samadhi is called 'cloud of virtue' in as much as it showers nectar drops of immortality through knowledge of Brahman, when all the hosts of Vasanas are entirely destroyed. The cloud of virtue is the name given to Samadhi in the Astanga Yoga of Patanjali.

Dharma shastras: Scriptures which set forth the rules for society and individuals, including spiritual observances. Manu Smriti is the most authoritative–and the foundation–of all the dharmashastras of India.

Dharmakaya: Reality; the Void; the Absolute; Sheath of the

Law–the Embodied Law.

Dharmashala: A place for pilgrims to stay, either free of charge or at a minimal cost.

Dharmi (1): One who follows dharma.

Dharmi (2): The substratum in which attributes or characteristics are seen to manifest or inhere.

Dharmic: Having to do with dharma; of the character of dharma.

Dhatu: Element; original element; core; constituent; the vital force in the human being by conserving which, through celibacy, the yogi develops ojas and tejas.

Dhira: Steadfast; strong; bold; courageous. One who possesses these qualities.

Dhoti: A long piece of material worn around the waist by traditionally-dressed men in India, rather like a long skirt.

Dhrita: Steadfastness; constancy; sustained effort; firmness; patience; endurance.

Dhriti: Steadfast; constant; sustaining effort; firm; patient; endurant.

Dhruva: A child who performed intense tapasya to attain the vision of Vishnu; permanent; fixed; steady.

Dhuni: A fire lighted by wandering monks, beside which they meditate and sleep.

Dhvani: Tone; sound; the subtle vibratory aspect of the vital shakti of the jiva.

Dvaita: Dual; duality; dualism.

Dhvani: Tone: sound; word; the subtle aspect of the vital shakti or the jiva in the vibrations.

Dhyana(m)/Dhyana Yoga: Meditation; contemplation.
Dhyanagamya: Attainable through meditation.
Dhyanika: Pertaining to dhyana or meditation.
Dhyatri: Meditator.
Dhyata: Meditator.
Dhyeya: Object of meditation or worship; purpose behind action.
Digambara: Naked; clad with the sky.
Diksha: Initiation.
Dina: Humble; helpless.
Dina bandhu: Friend of the Lowly; Friend of the poor and the helpless; a title of God.
Dinadayalu: Merciful towards the helpless.
Dipa: A wick lamp fed by oil or ghee; a flame in a lamp.
Dirgha: Long; prolonged; protracted.
Divya: Divine; divine nature; heavenly; celestial; sacred; luminous; supernatural.
Divyachakshu: Divine eye.
Divyachara: Conduct of the godly ones; a Tantric course of spiritual discipline meant for the pure and advanced aspirants.
Divyadrishti: Divine vision.
Diwali: The Hindu autumnal Festival of Lights celebrated everywhere in India and abroad.
Dosha: Defect; imperfection; blemish; fault; shortcoming. In Yoga philosophy there are five doshas: lust (kama), anger (krodha), greed (lobha), delusion (moha), and envy (matsarya).
Dosha drishti: Seeing defects; especially the defects in samsara

and samsaric life.

Drashta (1): Seer; perceiver; subject; a title of both the individual and the Supreme Selves or Purushas.

Drashta (2): The visible; the seen; that which is perceived.

Dravya: Substance.

Dridha: Firm; unshaken.

Dridhasushupti: Deep sleep state.

Dridhata: Firmness.

Drik: Seer; perceiver; vision.

Drishta: The visible; seen; that which is perceived.

Drishti: Seeing; sight; vision; view; opinion; gaze; perception.

Drishtisrishtivada: The doctrine holding that the existence of the world is purely the outcome of the faculty of perception, and that actually nothing exists beyond imagination.

Drishya(m): The seen; the object seen; the seeable; visible; perceptible; object of consciousness; nature; the world; that which can be seen by the physical sense.

Droha: Treachery; offence.

Dukha(m): Pain; suffering; misery; sorrow; grief; unhappiness; stress; that which is unsatisfactory.

Durbar: A royal court; a divine court of a god or goddess.

Durga: "Incomprehensible One;" "Difficult to reach;" the Universal Mother; she rides a lion (or tiger) and carries a weapon in each of her eight arms symbolizing the powers of the Self against ignorance and evil. She is invoked against all forms of evil–physical and metaphysical. Considered the consort, the shakti, of Shiva.

Dushkrita: Demerit; sin; evil action.

Duta: Messenger; ambassador; envoy; one who has been sent by another.

Dvaita: Dual; duality; dualism.

Dvaitadwaitavivarjita: Beyond monism and dualism; destitute of both oneness and two-ness or multiplicity.

Dvaita-bhava: Feeling of duality.

Dvaitavada: Dualism; the doctrine of dual existence propounded by Madhva.

Dwandwa(s): The pairs of opposites inherent in nature (prakriti) such as pleasure and pain, hot and cold, light and darkness, gain and loss, victory and defeat, love and hatred.

Dwandwata: State of duality.

Dwandvatita: Beyond the pairs of opposites, like heat and cold, hunger and thirst, pleasure and pain, etc.

Dwapara Yuga: See Yuga.

Dwesha: Aversion/avoidance for something, implying a dislike for it. This can be emotional (instinctual) or intellectual. It may range from simple non-preference to intense repulsion, antipathy and even hatred. See Raga.

Dwija: "Twice born;" any member of the three upper castes that has received the sacred thread (yajnopavita).

E

Eka(m): One.

Ekadashi: "The eleventh." The eleventh day of each half of the lunar month (that is, the eleventh day after the new and full moons) that is devoted to the worship of Vishnu and his avataras.

Ekadashi Vrata: Observing ekadhashi (the eleventh day after the new and full moons, sacred to Vishnu) by fasting–through abstinence from grains and other staples and eating much less than usual, oftentimes fasting from food (and sometimes water) until after sundown.

Ekagrata: One-pointedness of the mind; concentration.

Ekakshara: A common term for Om meaning "the Single Syllable" or "the Single Letter."

Ekam-evam-advitiyam: "One, only, without a second." A description of Brahman.

Ekanta: Solitude; seclusion.

Ekantabhava: Feeling of isolation or solitariness.

Ekantavada: Nondualism.

Ekantika: Final or ultimate; the Absolute.

Ekarasa: Homogeneous; uniform; one essence; Brahman.

Ekata: Oneness; homogeneity; absoluteness.

Ekatva: Unity; oneness.

Eknath: A renowned Vaishnava saint of Western India (Maharashtra).

Ekoham bahushyam: May I, the One, become many; this describes the primal idea which manifested itself from the One undivided Being prior to creation.

Evam: Thus; so; in this manner.

G

Gadi: Throne; seat; head (of a monastery).

Gagana: Sky; firmament.

Gaja: Elephant.

Gajanana Maharaj: Sri Gajanana Maharaj (Gajanan Murlidhar Gupte) of Nasik in western India (Maharashtra state) was a saint of the Nath Sampradaya in the first half of the twentieth century.

Gambhira: Deep; magnanimous; dignified; grand; imperious; grave.

Gana: One of a group of spirits that wander together–usually of various types. The term is also used as a kind of "miscellaneous" category for entities that have not otherwise been identified. A gana may be benevolent or malevolent, but is usually disorderly, chaotic, and wild in the sense of untamed or unruly, and potentially dangerous (hazardous). A gana's appearance is usually deformed, repulsive, or frightening. Shiva is said to be always accompanied by a group of devoted ganas.

Ganapati: "Lord of the Ganas" (the spirits that always

accompany Shiva). See Ganesha.

Ganapatya: A Hindu sect worshipping God as Ganpati (Ganesha); a member of this sect; pertaining to this sect.

Gandha: Smell; scent.

Gandharva: A demigod–a celestial musician and singer.

Ganesha: The elephant-headed son of Shiva and Parvati; the remover of obstacles; lord (pati) of the ganas (spirits that always accompany Shiva); god of wisdom; god of beginnings; the granter of success in spiritual and material life; in ritual worship he is worshipped first, and is therefore known as Adi-deva, the First God.

Ganga: See Ganges.

Ganges (Ganga): The sacred river–believed to be of divine origin–that flows from high up in the Himalayas, through the plains of Northern India, and empties into the Bay of Bengal. Hindus consider that bathing in the Ganges profoundly purifies both body and mind.

Ganja: Indian hemp; a form of marijuana found in India.

Garbha: Womb; belly; embryo; act of conception; inside, middle, or interior of anything; offspring of the sky.

Garuda: A great being who can assume bird form, and therefore considered the king of birds. Often depicted as an eagle, he is the vehicle of Vishnu.

Garva: Pride; egotism; arrogance.

Gaudapada: The guru of Shankara's guru, Govindapada.

Gauri: "The Golden One." A title of the Divine Mother, consort of Shiva.

Gayatri Mantra: A Rig Vedic mantra in the gayatri meter

invoking the solar powers of evolution and enlightenment, recited at sunrise and sunset.

Gayatri Meter: A meter found only in the Rig Veda, consisting of three lines of eight syllables each. It is considered especially appropriate for mantric invocation of deities before worship.

Gerua: The brownish-orange mud used to dye the clothing of Hindu monastics; the color produced by dyeing with gerua is also itself called gerua.

Ghat: A bathing-place: a stairway leading down to a river, pond, or water reservoir.

Ghatashuddi: "Purifying the pot." Purification of the physical body. An expression of Hatha Yoga, referring to the "earthen pot" of the body.

Ghee: Clarified butter.

Giri: Mountain; one of the ten branches of the Shankara Order.

Gita: Song; The Bhagavad Gita.

Gokul(a): The place of Krishna's childhood; Brindaban (Vrindavan).

Gokulashtami: Birthday of Krishna.

Gopala: "Cowherd;" a title of Krishna–both as baby and young boy.

Gopas: The cowherd boys of Vrindavan, playmates of Krishna.

Gopis: The milkmaids of Vrindavan, companions and devotees of Krishna.

Gopuram: A towerlike structure over an entrance (gateway) to a temple or temple compound, shaped like a wedge standing on its wide end, consisting of many tiers that are highly decorated (sculpted), often with images of deities and figures from Hindu cosmology.

Gorakhnath/Gorakshanath: A master yogi of the Nath Yogi (Nath Pantha) tradition. His dates are not positively known, but he seems to have lived for many centuries and travelled throughout all of India, Bhutan, Tibet, and Ladakh teaching philosophy and yoga.

Goshala: Cow shed.

Gotra: Clan; family; lineage.

Govinda: "Cowherd"–a title of Krishna.

Graha: Grip; grasp; planet; eclipse.

Granthi: Tie or knot.

Grihastha: One who is living in the second stage (ashrama) of Hindu social life; married householder's life.

Grihastya: The second stage (ashrama) of Hindu social life; married householder's life.

Guha/Guhya: Cave; secret; secret place; the heart (hridaya guha).

Guna: Quality, attribute, or characteristic arising from nature (Prakriti) itself; a mode of energy behavior. As a rule, when "guna" is used it is in reference to the three qualities of Prakriti, the three modes of energy behavior that are the basic qualities of nature, and which determine the inherent characteristics of all created things. They are: 1) sattwa–purity, light, harmony; 2) rajas–activity, passion; and 3) tamas–dullness, inertia, and ignorance.

Gunatita: Beyond the Gunas; one who has transcended & three Gunas.

Guni: Possessor of quality or qualities.

Guru: Teacher; preceptor; spiritual teacher or acharya.

Guru Dakshina: Gift given to the guru at the time of initiation.

Guru Nanak: Founder of the Sikh religion.

Gurukula: "Teacher's school" or "teacher's abode." A gurukula is the residence of a spiritual teacher where young students (brahmacharis) came to live and learn.

H

Hamsah: "I am He;" swan.

Hamsamantra: The Mantra "Soham" automatically and involuntarily uttered by the Jiva with every act of inspiration and expiration. See Ajapa Japa.

Hansa: Swan; see Hamsah.

Hanuman: A powerful monkey chief of extraordinary strength and prowess, whose exploits are celebrated in the epic Ramayana, the life of Rama. He was an ideal devotee (bhakta) and servant of Lord Rama.

Hara: "One who takes away;" a title of Shiva; the destroyer; the remover.

Hardwar: "The Gateway to Hari," a holy city in north-central India where the Ganges river flows into the plains.

Hari: Vishnu; "thief" in the sense of stealer of hearts.

Harikatha: Literally "Hari [Vishnu] Story," a Harikatha is a narration of the life and deeds of a deity or saint, interspersed with songs relevant to the events being spoken about or actual poetic reflections on those events and their significance. Kirtan is often a part, as well. This is the most popular and widespread traditional form of spiritual "entertainment."

Harsha: Exhilaration; joy.

Hatha Yoga: A system consisting of physical exercises, postures, and breathing exercises for gaining control over the physical body and prana.

Havishya: Sacrificial food. See Charu.

Havan: Fire sacrifice; yajna.

Hetu: Cause; reason.

Himsa: Injury, violence; killing.

Hiranyagarbha: Cosmic intelligence; the Supreme Lord of the universe; also called Brahma, cosmic Prana, Sutratma, Apara-brahman, Maha-brahma, or karya-brahman; Samasti-sukshma-sarirabhimani (the sum-total of all the subtle bodies); the highest created being through whom the Supreme Being projects the physical universe; cosmic mind.

Holy Mother: A reference to Sri Sarada Devi (Saradamani Mukhopadhyaya), the wife of Sri Ramakrishna, believed by many to have been an incarnation of the Divine Mother.

Homa: Vedic fire ritual/sacrifice.

Hri: Modesty; shame felt in doing wrong action.

Hridaya: Heart; essential center or core of something; essence; the Self.

Hridayagranthi: The knot of the heart, viz., avidya, kama, and karma.

Hridayaguha: The cave or chamber of the heart.

Hridayakamala: Lotus of the heart.

Hrishikesha: The bristling (or bushy) haired one. A title of Krishna.

I

Ichcha: Desire; will; wish; divine will; free will. From the verb root icch: "to wish," "to will."
Iccha Mrityu: Death at will.
Ichcha shakti: The power of desire; the power of the will; Shakti in the aspect of omnipotent Divine Will.
Ida: The subtle channel that extends from the base of the spine to the medulla on the left side of the spine.
Indra: King of the lesser "gods" (demigods); the ruler of heaven (Surendra Loka); the rain-god.
Indraloka: Indra's world; Indra's heaven.
Indriya: Organ. The five organs of perception (jnanendriyas) are the ear, skin, eye, tongue, and nose. The five organs of action (karmendriyas) are the voice, hand, foot, organ of excretion, and the organ of generation.
Isha: The Lord; Ishwara.
Isha Nath: The monastic name of Jesus of Nazareth in India as a member of the Nath Yogi Sampradaya.
Ishana: The all-enjoyer; Lord of everything; Lord of space; a name of Shiva.

Ishta: Object of desire.

Ishta-devata: Beloved deity. The deity preferred above all others by an individual. "Chosen ideal" is the usual English translation.

Ishta mantra: The mantra of the divine form specially beloved by an individual (ishta devata).

Ishtamurti: Favorite form or image of God.

Ishwara: "God" or "Lord" in the sense of the Supreme Power, Ruler, Master, or Controller of the cosmos. "Ishwara" implies the powers of omnipotence, omnipresence, and omniscience.

Ishwarakoti: Of the degree of God.

Ishwarapranidhana: Offering of one's life to God (Ishwara).

Ishwaraprayatna: God's will.

Ishwarapujanam: Worship of the Lord.

Ishwarasrishti: That which has been created by the Lord such as the elements, etc.

Ishwari: The Divine Cosmic Mother; the feminine form of Ishwara.

Iti: So; thus; this.

Itihasa: Epic; a book describing the life and adventures of a hero or heroes. The term is applied to Ramayana and the Mahabharata. The hero of the former is Sri Rama, the son of Dasaratha, and of the latter, the five Pandavas.

J

Jada: Inert; insentient; unconscious; matter.

Jada Bharata: A king of ancient India who became so fond of a deer that he was thinking of it intently at the time of death and was reborn as a deer though with full awareness of his previous life.

Jagadguru: World guru; world teacher.

Jadasamadhi: The state of Samadhi induced by the Hatha Yogic process in which there is no awareness or illumination as opposed to the Chaitanya Samadhi of the Vedantins.

Jagannath Puri: A pilgrim city on the east coast of India in Orissa State where multitudes come daily to worship Krishna in the temple of Jagannath (Lord of the World).

Jagat: World; cosmos; the ever-changing.

Jagradavastha: State of waking consciousness; consciousness of the objective universe.

Jagrat: The waking state.

Jagrita samadhi: Samadhi experienced in the waking state.

Jai: See Jaya.

Jala: Not real; a net; a snare; illusion.

Jamuna: A sacred river, tributary of the Ganges, which flows through Brindaban, the home of Lord Krishna in his childhood.

Janaka: The royal sage (raja rishi) who was the king of Mithila and a liberated yogi, a highly sought-after teacher of philosophy in ancient India. Sita, the wife of Rama, was his adopted daughter.

Janardana: Agitator of men (properly an epithet of Vishnu)–a title of Krishna.

Janardana Swami: A renowned saint of Western India (Maharashtra), a devotee of Lord Dattatreya.

Jani Janardan: God present in all human beings.

Janma: Birth; coming into being.

Janmashtami: Birthday of Krishna.

Janmotsava: Birthday celebration.

Japa: Repetition of a mantra.

Japa Mala: A string of beads, usually one hundred and eight, on which repetitions (japa) of a mantra are kept count of, or used just to help the yogi remember to do japa. Though one hundred and eight is the usual number of beads, smaller malas can be used when more convenient, especially since they can be put around the wrist when not in use. The beads can be of any substance, whatever is convenient or preferred.

Jara: Old age.

Jara-marana: Old age, decay, and death.

Jarayu: Womb.

Jata: Long matted hair.

Jati: Birth: species; class; creation.

Jatismara: Remembrance of the incidents of one's previous births (whether spontaneously or through special voluntary effort).

Jatyantaraparinama: Transformation of one genus or species into another.

Jaya: Victory; victorious; mastery; hail; salutations.

Jayanti: Birth day; victorious; conquering.

Jijnasa: Desire to know.

Jijnasu: One who aspires after knowledge; spiritual aspirant.

Jitendriya: One who has controlled the indriyas–the senses.

Jiva: Individual spirit.

Jivacaitanya: Individual consciousness.

Jivakoti: Belonging to the category or class of the individual soul.

Jivanmukta: One who is liberated here and now in this present life.

Jivanmukti: Liberation in this life.

Jivashrishti: That which has been created by the Jiva, viz., egoism, mine-ness, etc.

Jivatma(n): Individual spirit; individual consciousness.

Jiveshwarabhedha: Difference between the individual soul and God; the fundamental tenet of the dualistic school of thought.

Jnana: Knowledge; knowledge of Reality–of Brahman, the Absolute; also denotes the process of reasoning by which the Ultimate Truth is attained. The word is generally used to denote the knowledge by which one is aware of one's identity with Brahman.

Jnana kanda: The parts of the Veda dealing with the knowledge of the Absolute Brahman; the upanishads.

Jnana Marga: The path of discriminative knowledge leading to union with God.

Jnana Yoga: The path of knowledge; meditation through wisdom; constantly and seriously thinking on the true nature of the Self as taught by the upanishads.

Jnana yogi: One following the path of knowledge–jnana yoga.

Jnanabhyasa: A term generally used for the Vedantic mode of Sadhana.

Jnanacakshu: Eye of wisdom or eye of intuition.

Jnanagni: Fire of spiritual knowledge or wisdom.

Jnanakara: Of the form of wisdom; Brahman; sage.

Jnanakasha: The ether of knowledge; Brahman.

Jnanaloka: A particular region of the seven higher planes; just below Tapaloka.

Jnanamarga: The path of Knowledge; Jnana Yoga.

Jnanamaya: Full of knowledge.

Jnanamaya kosha: "The sheath of intellect (buddhi)." The level of intelligent thought and conceptualization. Sometimes called the Vijnanamaya kosha. The astral-causal body.

Jnananishtha: Established in the knowledge of the Self.

Jnanashakti: Power of knowing; the omnipotent universal force of knowledge.

Jnanayajna: Dissemination of knowledge; the Sadhana for, and the attainment of, knowledge, conceived of as an offering or divine sacrifice; offering of the individual to the Supreme.

Jnanendriyas: The five organs of perception: ear, skin, eye, tongue, and nose.

Jnaneshwar: A thirteenth-century saint of Maharashtra, a poet, philosopher and yogi of the Nath Yogi Panth or tradition.

Jnani: A follower of the path of knowledge (jnana); one who has realized–who knows–the Truth (Brahman).

Jnanodaya: Dawn of knowledge.

Jnanopadesha: Instruction in wisdom (jnana).

Jneya: Knowable; to be known.

Jyeshtha (1): The eldest; the best.

Jyeshtha (2): A star.

Jyoti(h): Light; flame; illumination; luminosity; effulgence.

Jyotisha: Astronomy; astrology.

Jyotirmaya: Full (mass) of light.

Jyotishmati: Effulgence; full of light.

Jyotiswarupa: Of the form of light.

K

Kabir: An Indian mystic of the fifteenth and sixteenth centuries.

Kala: Time measure, as in the time required to recite a mantra. It also sometimes means levels of creation or manifested beings.

Kailash(a): "Crystalline;" the name of the mountain home of Siva–a mountain peak in the Himalayas (in present-day Tibet) revered as the abode of Shiva, that is a famous place of pilgrimage.

Kaivalya: Transcendental state of Absolute Independence; state of absolute freedom from conditioned existence; moksha; isolation; final beatitude; emancipation.

Kaivalya-mukti (moksha): Liberation in which the yogi becomes one with Brahman while living (jivanmukti); final emancipation.

Kala (1): Time; death (or Yama); fate; black.

Kala (2): A unit of time; part; aspect; bit.

Kalachakra: The wheel of time.

Kalatita: Beyond time.

Kali: "The Black One;" the black-skinned goddess who

emerged from the body of Goddess Durga to defeat the demons that were attacking her. She wears a garland of skulls (or severed heads) around her neck and a skirt of severed arms–both symbolizing the sense of egotism. In one hand she wields the sword of spiritual wisdom (prajna) and in the other carries a severed head (ego). Despite her fearsome appearance, her two other hands are held in the gestures (mudras) that indicate: "Fear not" and "Draw near."

Kali Yuga: The dark age of spiritual and moral decline, said to be current now. See Yuga.

Kaliya: A monstrous serpent (cobra) that was killed by Krishna in his childhood.

Kalki: The future–tenth–incarnation (avatar) of Vishnu.

Kalpa: A Day of Brahma–4,320,000,000 years. It alternates with a Night of Brahma of the same length. He lives hundred such years. Brahma's life is known as Para, being of a longer duration than the life of any other being, and a half of it is called Parardha. He has now completed the first Parardha and is in the first day of the second Parardha. This day or Kalpa is known as Svetavarahakalpa. In the Day of Brahma creation is manifest and in the Night of Brahma is it resolved into its causal state.

Kalpana: Imagination of the mind; the association of name and permanence to objects; presumptive knowledge; assumption; creation.

Kalpanamatra: Mere imagination; lying only in imagination.

Kalpanika: That which is imagined; falsely created.

Kalpataru: "The wish-fulfilling tree." The celestial tree of

Hindu mythology, which grants all that a person standing or sitting under it desires.

Kalpita: Imaginary; created (artificial, unreal); dreamt.

Kalpita bheda: Imaginary difference.

Kalyana: Auspicious; blessed.

Kama: Desire; passion; lust.

Kamadeva: God of beauty and love; the Vedic Cupid who shoots a bow with flowers instead of arrows.

Kamadhenu: Wish-fulfilling cow produced at the churning of the milk ocean.

Kamadhuk: See Kamadhenu.

Kamagni: Fire of passion.

Kamajata: Born of desire or passion.

Kamakancana: Lust and wealth, the two great barriers to Self realization.

Kamamaya: Full of desire and lust.

Kamana: Longing; pleasure-seeking; cupidity.

Kamandalu: A water vessel carried by a traveling sannyasi; usually made of a gourd or coconut shell, it may also be earthenware. The kamandalu and staff (danda) are considered the insignia of the sannyasi along with gerua clothing.

Kamashakti: Force of lust or desire.

Kamasankalpa: Thought born of desire.

Kamyakarma: Any action done with desire for fruits thereof.

Kandarpa: See Kamadeva.

Kantha: Throat; neck.

Kapila: The great sage who formulated the Sankhya philosophy which is endorsed by Krishna in the Bhagavad Gita. (See the entry under Sankhya.)

Karana: "Instrument;" cause; instrumental cause; means of accomplishing something; reason. The means of knowledge and action. The inner and outer instruments (sense organs). The unmanifested potential cause that, in due time, takes shape as the visible effect; the material cause of the universe in such a state during the period of dissolution, i.e., cosmic energy in a potential condition.

Karana brahman: The highest and the first manifestation of the Absolute; the Absolute qualified by Maya; Saguna Brahman.

Karana-jagat: Causal world.

Karana sharira: The causal body (where the individual rests during sound, deep, dreamless sleep, the intellect, mind and senses being reduced to an unmanifested potential condition), also known as the anandamaya kosha, the "sheath of bliss."

Karanatma: The causal soul.

Karanavairagya: Dispassion caused through some misery, disappointment or failure in life.

Karanavastha: Causal state or condition.

Karatalabhiksha: Using hands (palms) as the begging bowl.

Karika: Commentary; treatise.

Karma: Karma, derived from the Sanskrit root *kri*, which means to act, do, or make, means any kind of action, including thought and feeling. It also means the effects of action. Karma is both action and reaction, the metaphysical equivalent of the principle: "For every action there is an equal and opposite reaction." "Whatsoever a man soweth, that shall he also reap" (Galatians 6:7). It is karma operating through the law of cause and effect that binds the jiva or the individual soul to the wheel of birth and death. There are three forms of karma: sanchita, agami, and prarabdha. Sanchita karma is the vast store of accumulated actions done in the past, the fruits of which have not yet been reaped. Agami karma is the action that will be done by the individual in the future. Prarabdha karma is the action that has begun to fructify, the fruit of which is being reaped in this life.

Karma Marga: The path of selfless action leading to union with God.

Karma Yoga: The Yoga of selfless (unattached) action; performance of one's own duty; service of humanity.

Karma Yogi: One who practices karma yoga.

Karmabandhanam: Karmic bondage; karmic tie.

Karmabhumi: Land of action; the earth-plane; the world of karma, where karma is sown and reaped.

Karmadhyaksha: Controller or ruler of actions; God; soul.

Karmaja: Born of action or Prarabdha.

Karmakanda: The ritual portion of the Veda. The philosophy that Vedic ritual is the only path to perfection.

Karmakandi(n): One who follows the Karma-kanda as philosophy and practice.

Karmapara: Dependent on karma.

Karmaphala: The fruit of actions; the consequence of a deed.

Karmasakshi: Witness of actions.

Karmashaya: The receptacle or mass of karmas; aggregate of works done; latent impressions of action which will eventually fructify.

Karmavada: The doctrine of karma upholding that each deed, good or bad, is inevitably followed by pleasure or pain as its sure effect.

Karmendriyas: The five organs of action: voice, hand, foot, organ of excretion, and the organ of generation.

Karmic: Having to do with karma.

Karta: The doer, the agent–specifically, of action.

Kartavya: Duty; that which is to be done or ought to be done.

Kartritva: Doership; agency of action.

Kartrivada: The claim of being an independent doer.

Karttikeya: See Subramanya.

Karuna: Mercy; compassion; kindness.

Karya: Effect (correlative of Karana); the physical body is described as the Karya, in contrast to the causal body, the Karana; the world; Hiranyagarbha.

Karyam: "To-be-done;" to be performed; a duty.

Kashaya: Attachment to worldly objects; passion; emotion; the subtle influence in the mind produced by enjoyment and left there to fructify in time to come and distract the mind from samadhi; hidden impressions.

Kashi: Varanasi (Benares).

Kaupina: A small strip of cloth used to cover one's private parts. Also called a langoti.

Kauravas: The opponents of the Pandavas in the Mahabharata War, led by Duryodhana.

Katha: Tale or story; history or narrative.

Kaviraj: Ayurvedic physician.

Kaya: Physical body.

Kayastha: A kayastha is a member of the Kayastha caste that is traditionally believed to be been keepers of public records and accounts, writers and state administrators. Yet their actual place in the caste system has never been really determined. In north central India the term "Kayastha" is a polite and non-commital term used to refer to non-Brahmins.

Kedarnath (Kedar Nath): One of the chief places of pilgrimage in India: a temple on a mountaintop in the Himalayas, dedicated to the worship of Shiva in the form of a linga installed there by Adi Shankaracharya.

Kendra: Centre; heart.

Keshava: Handsome-haired one–a title of Krishna.

Kevala: Oneness; alone; single; independent; perfect; uncompounded. The Absolute.

Kevala-advaita: Absolute Non-dualism culminating in liberation.

Kevala Advaitin: A nondualist intent on the attainment of the state of Kaivalya–liberation.

Kevala kumbhaka: Sudden restraint of breath, not preceded by either inhalation or exhalation. Spontaneous breath retention, the kumbhaka which occurs during samadhi.

Kha: Sky; ether.

Khechara: What moves in the sky; the celestial being or the bird.

Khechari Mudra: "Sky-walking" mudra that enables the yogi to "move" in (or expand into) the Chidakasha. There are two forms of Khechari Mudra. In Hatha Yoga it is the insertion of the tip of the tongue into the nasal cavity above the upper palate. In meditation (Dhyana Yoga) it is the gentle turning upward of the eyes as though looking at a point far distant.

Khol: Collyrium. A black substance put around the eyes. Though used cosmetically, it is considered to have medicinal properties that protect the eyes from infection or disease. It is often put around children's eyes for this purpose.

Khol: See Mridangam.

Khyati: Apprehension; discernment; knowledge; vision.

Kinnara: A celestial musician.

Kirtan(a): Singing the names and praises of God; devotional chanting.

Kirti: Fame; reputation.

Klesha: Literally, taints or afflictions; pain. The kleshas are: ignorance, egotism, attractions and repulsions towards objects, and desperate clinging to physical life from the fear of death. (See Yoga Sutras 2:2-9.)

Klishta: Afflicted, painful or pain-bearing.

Kosha: Sheath; bag; scabbard; a sheath enclosing the soul; body. There are five such concentric sheaths or bodies: the sheaths of bliss, intellect, mind, life-force and the physical body–the anandamaya, jnanamaya, manomaya, pranamaya and annamaya bodies respectively.

Krama: Order; sequence; sequential order or progression; stage; underlying process; natural law–all these are inherent in their substratum or dharmi.

Krama mukti: Attainment of liberation in stages; gradual liberation; passing from this world to a higher world beyond rebirth and from there attaining liberation.

Kratu: Action; plan; intention; desire; applied will; intelligence personified; conviction; purpose; determination; a firm belief; inspiration; enlightenment; sacrificial rite or ceremony; sacrifice; yajna; offering; worship, resolution. *Bhadra kratu:* right judgment; good understanding.

Kripa: Grace; mercy; compassion; blessing. There are three kinds of kripa: 1) sadhana kripa, the grace of self-effort; 2) guru kripa, the grace of a teacher, and 3) divya kripa, divine grace.

Krishna: An avatar born in India about three thousand years ago, Whose teachings to His disciple Arjuna on the eve of the Great India (Mahabharata) War comprise the Bhagavad Gita.

Krishnarpana: That which has been offered to Krishna, to God.

Krishnadvaipayana: The famous Vyasa, the writer of the Mahabharata, eighteen Puranas, and the compiler of the Vedas.

Kritabuddhi: (Very) intelligent; rational; discriminative.

Kritakritya: One who has done all actions, i.e., jnani.

Kritatma: Pure soul who is extremely good and extremely self-sacrificing.

Kriya: Purificatory action, practice, exercise, or rite; action; activity; movement; function; skill. Kriyas purify the body and nervous system as well as the subtle bodies to enable the yogi to reach and hold on to higher levels of consciousness and being.

Kriya Shakti: The power or faculty of action.

Kriya Yoga: The Yoga of Purification: "Austerity (tapasya), self-study (swadhyaya), and offering of the life to God (Ishwara pranidhana) are Kriya Yoga" (Yoga Sutras 2:1).

Kriyamana: Literally: "what is being done;" the effect of the deeds of the present life to be experienced in the future; same as Agami.

Krodha: Anger, wrath; fury.

Krurata: Cruelty; pitilessness.

Kshama: Forgiveness; patience; forbearance.

Kshara: World; perishable.

Kshatriya: A member of the ruler/warrior caste.

Kshaya: Destruction; thinning; diminishing; annihilation.

Kshetra: A holy place; field; also physical body in the philosophical sense.

Kshetrajna: The individual or the Supreme Soul.

Kshudha: Hunger.

Kubera: The god of wealth.

Kukarma: Negative, bad or evil action.

Kula: Possessing a form.

Kulakundalini: The primordial cosmic energy located in the individual.

Kumar(a): A male virgin.

Kumaras (Four): At the beginning of this creation cycle the four most advanced human souls (Sanaka, Sanandana,

Sanatkumara and Sanatsujata) from the previous cycle refused to engage in the creation of the world and to enter into worldly life despite the command of Brahma that they do so. Instead they engaged in intense yoga and attained liberation. The chief of these was Sanatkumara who thereby became the Lord of Liberation for all humanity. Ever present in subtle form, Sanatkumara assists those who truly seek liberation–usually invisibly and unknown to them. But at their attainment of perfect realization he reveals himself to them and leads them to the worlds beyond compulsory rebirth.

Kumari: A female virgin; a formal title of address for an unmarried woman.

Kumari Puja: The worship of a virgin (usually a prepubescent girl) as an embodiment of the Divine Mother.

Kumbha: Pot; water vessel.

Kumbhaka: Retention of breath; suspension of breath.

Kumkum: Red-colored powder used for making a ritual mark between the eyebrows.

Kund: A pond; a small natural bathing place.

Kundalini: The primordial cosmic conscious/energy located in the individual; it is usually thought of as lying coiled up like a serpent at the base of the spine.

Kusha: One of the varieties of sacred grass (darbha) used in many religious rites. Because of its insulating qualities, both physical and metaphysical, it is recommended as a seat (asana) for meditation, and as mats for sleeping (it keeps the sleeper warm).

Kutastha: Immutable; absolutely changeless; not subject to change; literally: "summit abiding" or "on the summit." He who is found without exception in all creatures from Brahma or the creator down to ants and Who is shining as the Self and dwells as witness to the intellect of all creatures; rock-seated; unchanging; another name for Brahman.

Kutastha chaitanya: Inner Self; individual Consciousness destitute of egoism.

Kutir(a): Hut; cottage; house; building; hermitage.

L

Laghava: Lightness of body through practice of meditation.

Laghima: Lightness; one of the eight major Siddhis of Yoga practice.

Lahiri Mahasaya: Shyama Charan Lahiri, one of the greatest yogis of nineteenth-century India, written about extensively in *Autobiography of a Yogi* by Paramhansa Yogananda.

Lajja: Shame; shyness.

Lakh: One hundred thousand.

Lakshana: Definition; characteristic; condition; attribute; sign; mark.

Lakshmana: The brother of Rama whom he accompanied into exile.

Lakshmi: The consort of Vishnu; the goddess of wealth and prosperity.

Lakshya: Perceivable object; object or point of concentration-attention; target; vision.

Lalla Yogeshwari: A great fourteenth century Kashmiri yogini and mystic, the first poet in the Kashmiri language, whose mystic verses called Vakhs are popular even today.

Langoti: See kaupina.
Laya: Dissolution; merging.
Laya Yoga: Dissolution; merging; process of absorption of the individual soul into the Supreme Sou; another name of Nada-yoga or Kundalini-yoga.
Layachintana: Concentration of the mind with a view to dissolve it; meditation where the mind is carried on progressively from grosser to subtler ideas until it is dissolved in the Unmanifested or Para Brahman.
Lila: Play; sport; divine play; the cosmic play. The concept that creation is a play of the divine, existing for no other reason than for the mere joy of it. The life of an avatar is often spoken of as lila.
Linga: Mark; gender; sign; symbol. Usually a reference to a column-like or egg-shaped symbol of Shiva.
Lingadeha: The astral body; the subtle body.
Lingasharira: Subtle body; astral body (also called sukshma-sharira); the subtle or psychic body that becomes particularly active during the dream-state by creating a world of its own; the three sheaths of intelligence, mind and vital energy constitute this body.
Lingatman: The subtle self.
Lobha: Greed; covetousness.
Loka: World or realm; sphere, level, or plane of existence, whether physical, astral, or causal.
Lokaishana: Desire for fame.
Lokapala: The ruler, overseer or guardian of a loka.
Lokasangraha: Solidarity of the world; uplift of the world.

Loluta: Covetousness; cupidity; earthly enjoyment.
Lota: A metal water vessel used for drinking, carrying, or pouring water.

M

Ma: Momma.

Mada: Pride; arrogance.

Madhava: Descendant of Madhu (a Yadava or Madhava patriarch). A title of Krishna.

Madhavacharya: The thirteenth century Vaishnava founder and expounder of the Dvaita (Dualist) Vedanta philosophy.

Madhu: Honey; sweet substance; sweet.

Madhukari bhiksha: Alms collected from door to door like a bee collecting honey from flower to flower.

Madhuparka: An offering for the Lord containing honey, curd, etc.

Madhura: The attitude of a devotee expressing the emotion that exists between a lover and the beloved; the devotee looks upon God as his Beloved.

Madhusudana: Destroyer of the Demon Madhu (properly an epithet of Vishnu)–a title of Krishna

Madhyama: Moderate; the middle stage of sound as it develops from silent to fully audible or spoken. Sound in its subtle form as it exists in the mind/psyche before its gross manifestation.

Maha: A prefix meaning "great," the root of the Latin word magna.

Mahabhava: Supreme love and yearning for God, exemplified by Sri Radha.

Mahabharata: The world's longest epic poem (110,00 verses) about the Mahabharata (Great Indian) War that took place about three thousand years ago. The Mahabharata also includes the Bhagavad Gita, the most popular sacred text of Hinduism.

Mahabhutas: The Five Elements (Panchabhuta): ether (akasha), air (vayu), fire (agni), water(ap), and earth (prithvi).

Mahabodha: The Great Awakening.

Mahadbrahma: Hiranyagarbha; Sutratma; cosmic intelligence.

Mahadeva: "The Great God;" a title of Shiva.

Mahakalpa: The great cycle; hundred years of Brahma when the whole universe is dissolved in the Unmanifested.

Mahamantra: "The Great Mantra," popularly known in the United States and Europe as "the Hare Krishna Mantra"– Hare Rama, Hare Rama, Rama, Rama, Hare, Hare; Hare Krishna, Hare Krishna, Krishna, Krishna, Hare, Hare.

Mahamaya: "Great illusion;" divine Power operating as identified with the Supreme Lord. A title of Shakti, the Goddess.

Mahamrityunjaya: "The Great Conqueror of Death." A title and four-armed form of Shiva.

Mahamrityunjaya mantra: "The Great Conqueror of Death Mantra." A Vedic verse addressed to Shiva that is recited for protection, recovery from disease, and extension of life.

Mahan: The Great; the evolute from Prakriti according to the Sankhya; Brahma or Hiranyagarbha.

Mahant: The head of an ashram; an abbot.

Mahapralaya: The final cosmic dissolution; the dissolution of all the worlds of relativity (Bhuloka, Bhuvaloka, Swaloka, Mahaloka, Janaloka, Tapaloka, and Satyaloka), until nothing but the Absolute remains. There are lesser dissolutions, known simply as pralayas, when only the first five worlds (lokas) are dissolved.

Mahaprana: The undifferentiated, intelligent cosmic life-force that becomes the five pranas; all things contain the mahaprana and are manifestations of the mahaprana; the dynamic aspect of universal Consciousness; the superconscious Divine Life in all things.

Mahapurusha: Great being; great soul; a person of supreme spiritual character and realization; a sage; the Supreme Lord.

Maharaj(a): "Great king;" lord; master; a title of respect used to address holy men.

Maharashtra: One of the largest–and the wealthiest–states in India, whose capital is Mumbai (Bombay).

Marathi: The language of Maharashtra.

Maharatha: "A great-car-warrior," a commander of eleven thousand bowmen as he rode in his chariot.

Maharloka: The fourth of the seven planes above the nether regions.

Mahar(i)shi: Maha-rishi–great sage.

Mahasamadhi: Literally "the great union [samadhi]," this refers to a realized yogi's conscious departure from the physical body at death.

Mahashakti: The Great Power; the divine creative energy.

Mahashivaratri: "The Great Night of Shiva." The major, night-long festival of the worship of Shiva that occurs on the fourteenth day of the dark half of the lunar month known as Phalguna (usually in February, but every third year when an extra month is added to the lunar calendar, it may occur in March).

Mahat: Great; the first product from Prakriti in evolution, according to Sankhya philosophy; intellect; the principle of intelligence or Buddhi; Hiranyagarbha or Brahma.

Mahat Tattwa: The Great Principle; the first product from Prakriti in evolution; intellect. The principle of Cosmic Intelligence or Buddhi; universal Christ Consciousness, the "Son of God," the "Only Begotten of the Father," "the firstborn of every creature."

Mahatahparah: Beyond the great; greater than the great; above the reach of the intellect.

Mahatma: Literally: "a great soul [atma]." Usually a designation for a sannyasi, sage or saint.

Mahattva: Greatness.

Mahavakya: Literally: "Great Saying." The highest Vedantic truth, found in the Upanishads expressing the highest Vedantic truths or the identity between the individual soul and the Supreme Soul. There are four Mahavakyas: 1) Prajñanam Brahma–"Consciousness is Brahman" (Aitareya Upanishad 3.3); 2) Ayam Atma Brahma–"This Self is Brahman" (Mandukya Upanishad 1.2); 3) Tat Twam

Asi–"Thou art That" (Chandogya Upanishad 6.8.7); 4) Aham Brahmasmi–"I am Brahman" (Brihadaranyaka Upanishad 1.4.10).

Mahayoga: Great yoga.

Mahayogi: Great yogi.

Maheshwara: The Great Ishwara (Lord); Shiva.

Mahima (1): Greatness; glory; magnification; extensive magnitude; miracle.

Mahima (2): The psychic power (siddhi) to become as large as desired.

Mahout: Trainer-handler of an elephant.

Maitreya/Maitri: Friendliness; friendship; love.

Maithuna(m): Sexual intercourse.

Mala (1): Garland; flower garland; rosary; chain.

Mala (2): Taint; impurity; defilement; defect; ignorance, limitation of consciousness.

Malina: Impure; defective.

Mamakara: Mine-ness; the thought "this is mine" in relation to the body and the things connected with it, such as wife, children, relations,, friends, home, wealth and the like.

Mamata: Mine-ness.

Mana: Respect; sense of self-respect.

Manahkalpitajagat: The world created by the mind or imagination.

Manahshuddhi: Purification of the mind.

Manana: Thinking, pondering, reflecting, considering.

Manana shakti: Power of reflection and concentration.

Manas(a): The sensory mind; the perceiving faculty that

receives the messages of the senses.

Manasahmanah: Mind of mind; the Inner Ruler or the Self or Brahman.

Manasa puja: Mental worship; an item of ritualistic worship requiring the devotee to go mentally through the entire procedure of worship.

Manasarovar: A sacred lake near Mount Kailash the abode of Shiva. Pilgrims not only bathe in the lake on the way to Kailash, they often see visions in its water, hence the name "Lake of the Mind." The present Dalai Lama was found through visions seen in Manasarovar.

Manasic/Manasika: Mental; having to do with the mind (manas).

Manasika japa: Mental repetition of a Mantra.

Manasika kriya: Mental action.

Manashi shakti: Power of mind; standing.

Manava: Man; a human being; a descendant of Manu.

Manava dharma: The essential nature of man; religion of man; the duties of man.

Mandala: Region; sphere or plane, e.g., Suryamandala or the solar region.

Mandir(a): Temple; abode.

Mangala: Auspicious.

Mangalarati: See Arati.

Manipura chakra: Energy center located in the spine at the point opposite the navel. Seat of the Fire element.

Manisha: Independent power of thinking.

Manodharma: Natural attributes or properties of the mind.

Manojaya: Conquest of the mind.

Manolaya: Involution and dissolution of the mind into its cause.

Manomatrajagat: Mind alone is world; world made up of mind only.

Manomaya kosha: "The sheath of the mind (manas–mental substance)." The level (kosha) of the sensory mind. The astral body.

Manonasha: Destruction of the mind.

Manonirodha: Control or annihilation of the mind.

Manorajya: Building castles in the air; mental kingdom.

Manoratha: Desire of the mind.

Mantra(m): Sacred syllable or word or set of words through the repetition and reflection of which one attains perfection or realization of the Self. Literally, "a transforming thought" (manat trayate). A mantra, then is a sound formula that transforms the consciousness.

Mantra Yoga: The Yoga of the Divine Word; the science of sound; the path to divine union through repetition of a mantra–a sound formula that transforms the consciousness.

Mantra chaitanya: The dormant potency of a Mantra.

Mantra shakti: Power of the Lord's Name; the potency of any Mantra.

Mantra siddhi: Perfection in the practice of Mantra-Japa; mastery over the Devata of a Mantra so that the Devata graces the votary whenever invoked.

Mantric: Having to do with mantra(s)–their sound or their power.

Manu: The ancient lawgiver, whose code, The Laws of Manu (Manu Smriti) is the foundation of Hindu religious and social conduct.

Manus: Progenitors of the human race who were also its lawgivers and teachers.

Manusha(m): Human being; humanity.

Mara: The embodiment of the power of cosmic evil, illusion, and delusion; Satan.

Marathi: The language of Maharashtra.

Mardava: Mildness; tenderness; smoothness.

Marga: Way; path; road; street; approach to God-realization (bhakti marga, jnana marga, karma marga, yoga marga, etc.).

Margashirsha: A lunar month, roughly the latter half of November and the first half of December. This is the time of ideal weather in India.

Marichi: The chief of the Maruts.

Martanda: The Sun-God.

Maruts: The presiding deities of winds and storms.

Math: A monastery.

Mata: Mother.

Mati: Thought; view; opinion; faith; religion; doctrine; tradition; conviction; mind rightly directed towards knowledge revealed and practice enjoined by the shastras.

Matra: Letters of the alphabet or their sounds; mode; measure; unit; prosodial instant–the length of time required for pronouncing a short vowel.

Matrika: Letter or sound syllable which is the basis of all words and hence of all knowledge; "little mothers."

Matsarya: jealousy.

Martyaloka: The mortal world; earth-plane.

Matsyendranath: Guru of Gorakhnath and the first publicly known Nath Yogi, having become a disciple of Adinath who is considered an avatar of Shiva. As with Gorakhnath, we have no dates for him.

Mauna(m): Silence–not speaking.

Maya: The illusive power of Brahman; the veiling and the projecting power of the universe, the power of Cosmic Illusion. "The Measurer"–a reference to the two delusive "measures," Time and Space.

Mayamohajala: The jugglery or deception set by the infatuation of Maya.

Mayashabalabrahma: Another name for Saguna Brahman or Ishvara (the Brahman conjoined with attributes, enwrapped in and coloured with Maya.)

Mayavada: Also known as Mithyavada; theory of illusion; doctrine of the phenomenal character of the universe.

Mayavi: Master-magician; great juggler; Brahman.

Mayic: Having to do with Maya.

Medha: Power of retaining the import of studies; intelligence or intellect; power of understanding.

Meru: The mountain, of supreme height, on which the gods dwell, or the mountain on which Shiva is ever seated in meditation, said to be the center of the world, supporting heaven itself–obviously a yogic symbol of the spinal column or merudanda. The name of the central bead on a japa mala (rosary).

Merudanda: The spinal column in yogic symbolism; see Meru.

Mimamsa: An enquiry into the nature of a thing; the science of philosophical logic enquiring into Vedic knowledge. Usually a reference to Purva-Mimamsa, one of the six schools of orthodox Indian philosophy. It focuses on the Vedas and the Vedic rites to establish their supreme spiritual value and authority.

Mimamsaka: A follower of the Purva Mimamsa school of philosophy. See Mimamsa.

Mirabai: A sixteenth-century Rajasthani princess, whose devotional songs are among the greatest written in India.

Mitahara: Moderate diet.

Mithya: Not real; neither real nor unreal; illusory; false; untrue; incorrect.

Mithyabhimana: False egoism.

Mithyachara: Sinful conduct; hypocrisy.

Mithyadrishti: The vision that this world is unreal.

Mithyahamkara: Same as Mithyabhimana.

Mithyajnana: False knowledge.

Mithyasambandha: False relationship.

Mithyavada: Phenomenal doctrine; theory of illusion.

Mleccha: Foreigner; an alien; barbarian; non-Aryan.

Moha: Delusion–in relation to something, usually producing delusive attachment or infatuation based on a completely false perception and evaluation of the object.

Mohana: Fascination.

Moksha: Release; liberation; the term is particularly applied to the liberation from the bondage of karma and the wheel of birth and death; Absolute Experience.

Mridanga(m): A drum used exclusively in devotional music, also known as a khol.

Mridu: Mild.

Mrisha: Vain; hollow; false; unreal.

Mrita(m): Dead.

Mrityu(h): Death; of death; a title of Yama, the Lord of Death.

Mrityum: Death.

Mrityunjaya: Conquerer of death; one of the names of Lord Siva.

Mudhavastha: State of ignorance or forgetfulness of one's real nature.

Mudita: Complacency; joy; happiness.

Mudra: A position–usually of the hands/fingers–which inherently produces a desired state in the subtle energy levels (prana) according to the Tantric system; a Hatha Yoga posture; a position of the eyes in meditation.

Muhurta: A unit of time–a thirtieth part of a day, forty-eight minutes in length; auspicious moment.

Mukta: One who is liberated–freed–usually in the sense of one who has attained moksha or spiritual liberation.

Mukta purusha: A person liberated from all kinds of bondage; One freed from birth and death.

Mukti: Moksha; liberation.

Mula: Origin(al); primary; root; base.

Mulachaitanya: Root consciousness; seed of the creation.

Muladhara chakra: "Seat of the root." Energy center located at the base of the spine. Seat of the Earth element.

Mulajnana: Primal ignorance which contains all potentialities.

Mulamantra: Root Mantra; the powerful and the most important of the Mantras of any deity.

Mulaprakriti: Avyaktam; the Root [Basic] Energy from which all things are formed. The Divine Prakriti or Energy of God.

Mulashakti: Root power or energy; Mulaprakriti.

Mumukshu: Seeker after liberation (moksha).

Mumukshutwa: Intense desire or yearning for liberation (moksha).

Muni: "Silent one" (one observing the vow of silence–mauna); sage; ascetic.

Murti: Image; statue; idol; figure; embodiment.

N

Nada: Sound; the resonance of sound; mystic inner sound; the primal sound or first vibration from which all creation has emanated; the first manifestation of the unmanifested Absolute; Omkara or Shabda Brahman; the inner sound of a mantra experienced in meditation.

Nadi: A channel in the subtle (astral) body through which subtle prana (psychic energy) flows; a physical nerve. Yoga treatises say that there are seventy-two thousand nadis in the energy system of the human being.

Nadi shuddhi: Purification of the Nadis.

Naga: Snake; naked; a kind of powerful spirit-being worshipped in some areas of India, possessing great psychic powers and the ability to appear and communicate with human beings; one order of Sadhus, who are nude.

Nagar(a): City; town.

Nagar(san)kirtan: Kirtan done in procession through the streets or sometimes within or around an ashram or other property.

Nagas: Astral beings that often interact with human beings, usually taking the form of snakes. (In Sanskrit naga is the word for snake.)

Nahabat: A temple music tower. Musicians sit on the upper story and play during festivals and sometimes at the time of daily worship. Holy Mother Sarada Devi lived in the northern nahabat of the Dakshineshwar Kali Temple.

Naishthika brahmachari: One who has taken the vow of life-long celibacy; a permanent brahmachari.

Naivedya: Edible offerings to the deity in a temple or household shrine.

Nama: Name. The Divine Name.

Nama-rupa: Name and form; the nature of the world.

Namaskara: "I bow to you;" a respectful greeting.

Namasmarana: Remembrance (repetition) of the Name of God. Remembrance of the Lord through repetition of His name.

Namrata: Humility.

Nanak (Guru): Founder of the Sikh religion in the fifteenth century.

Narada: A primeval sage to whom some of the verses of the Rig Veda are attributed.

Naraka: Hell. In Sanatana Dharma's cosmology there are many hells according to the karma of those dwelling in them before being reincarnated.

Niranjana: Without blemish; spotless; stainless; untainted; pure; simple; void of passion or emotion; a title of Brahman.

Narasingha (Narasimha): The fourth avatara of Vishnu in the form of a man with the head of a lion.

Narayana: A proper name of God–specifically of Vishnu. The term by etymology means a Being that supports all things, that is reached by them and that helps them to do so; also one who pervades all things. He Who dwells in man. Literally: "God in humanity." Sadhus often address one another as Narayana and greet one another: "Namo Narayanaya"–I salute Narayana [in you].

Narayana shila: See Shalagrama.

Nasika: Nose; the subtle organ of smell corresponding to the outer organ, the nose.

Nasikagram: The origin of the nose (nasik). *Agram* means beginning, top, tip and the nearest end. Although in translations of texts such as the Bhagavad Gita (6:13), "tip [end] of the nose" is often the translation of nasikagram, some yogis insist that the top of the nose is meant and that the eyes must be turned upward in meditation. This is in harmony with Bhagavad Gita 5:27 where the yogi is told to turn up the eyes toward the two eyebrows.

Nasikagradrishti: Gaze at the origin of the nose.

Nataraja: "King of the Dance," a title of Shiva the Cosmic Dancer. The whole creation is the dance of Shiva.

Nath(a): Master; lord; ruler; protector.

Nath Pantha (Nathas): Various associations of yogis who trace their roots back to Matsyendranath and the Nath Yogi Sampradaya.

Nath Yogi: A member of the Nath Yogi Sampradaya.

Nath Yogi Sampradaya: An ancient order of yogis claiming Matsyendranath, Gorakhnath, Patanjali, Jnaneshwar and

Jesus (Isha Nath) among their master teachers.

Navadhvara kuti: The nine-gated house–the body.

Navadhvara puri: The nine-gated city–the body.

Neem Karoli Baba: One of India's most amazing and mysterious spiritual figures. The life of this great miracle-worker and master spanned from two to four centuries (at the least), including most of the twentieth century.

Neti-neti: "Not this, not this." The way of describing the indescribable Brahman by enumerating what It is not; the analytical process of progressively negating all names and forms, in order to arrive at the eternal underlying Truth.

Nididhyasana: Meditation; contemplation; profound and continuous meditation. It is a continuous, unbroken stream of ideas of the same kind as those of the Absolute. It removes the contrariwise tendencies of the mind.

Nidra: Sleep; either dreaming or deep sleep state; also a name of Yogamaya.

Nigrahas: Restraint; control; subduing.

Nija: Perception without sense organs.

Nijananda: The bliss beyond sense perception.

Nimitta: Cause; instrument; effect; sign; substance.

Nine Nathas: Nine great Masters of the Nath Yogi Sampradaya, including Matsyendranath and Ghoraknath.

Nirakara: Without form.

Niralamba: Supportless.

Niramaya: Without disease, defect or deficiency; health; complete; entire; pure.

Niranjana: Without blemish; spotless.

Niratisaya: Unsurpassed.

Niratisaya Ananda: Eternal, infinite bliss; the highest bliss above which bliss there is none other.

Nirbhaya: Fearless.

Nirbija: "Without seed;" without attributes; without the production of samskaras or subtle karmas.

Nirbija samadhi: Nirvikalpa samadhi wherein the seeds of samskaras or karmas are destroyed ("fried" or "roasted") by Jnana, and which produces no samskaras or karmas.

Nirdwandwa: Beyond the pairs of opposites such as pleasure and pain.

Nirguna: Without attributes or qualities (gunas).

Nirguna Brahman: The impersonal, attributeless Absolute beyond all description or designation.

Nirmala: Without impurity; pure; without defect or blemish.

Nirodha: Restraint; restriction; suppression; dissolving/dissolution; cessation; disappearance; control inhibition; annihilation; process of ending.

Nirupadhika: Unconditioned; without any limiting adjunct.

Nirvana: Liberation; final emancipation; the term is particularly applied to the liberation from the bondage of karma and the wheel of birth and death that comes from knowing Brahman; Absolute Experience. See Moksha.

Nirvana chakra: Energy center located beneath the crown of the head and opposite the middle of the forehead–in the midst of the brain.

Nirveda(m): Complete indifference; disregard of worldly objects.

Nirvedya: Unknowable.

Nirvichara samadhi: A stage in samadhi wherein the mind (chitta) no longer identified with a subtle object or assumes its form, simply resting in perception without analytical awareness of its nature by means of the buddhi, whose operation has become completely suspended so that only pure awareness remains; without deliberation and reasoning or inquiry.

Nirvikalpa: Indeterminate; non-conceptual; without the modifications of the mind; beyond all duality.

Nirvikalpa samadhi: Samadhi in which there is no objective experience or experience of "qualities" whatsoever, and in which the triad of knower, knowledge and known does not exist; purely subjective experience of the formless and qualitiless and unconditioned Absolute. The highest state of samadhi, beyond all thought, attribute, and description.

Nirvikara: Without transformation, modifications, or change; changeless.

Nirvitarka Samadhi: Union with an object in which remembrance of their names and qualities is not present. (See Vitarka.)

Nishkama: Free from wish or desire; desirelessness; selfless, unselfish; action without expectation of fruits.

Nishkama bhava: Motiveless, spontaneous feeling; the attitude of non-expectation of fruits of action.

Nishkama karma: Desireless action; disinterested action; action dedicated to God without personal desire for the fruits of the action; selfless action.

Nishkama Karma Yoga: Action without expectation of fruits, and done without personal interest or egoism.

Nishtha: Steadfastness; establishment in a certain state.

Nitya: Eternal; permanent; unchanging; the ultimate Reality; the eternal Absolute. Secondarily: daily or obligatory as in Nityakarma.

Nityakarma: Daily obligatory rite, as Sandlayavandana, etc.

Nityamukta: Eternally free.

Nityananda (Paramhansa): A great Master of the nineteenth and twentieth centuries, and the most renowned Nath Yogi of our times. His *Chidakasha Gita* contains some of the most profound statements on philosophy and yoga.

Nityashuddha: Eternally pure.

Nityayukta: Eternally united (with the Absolute).

Nivritti: Negation; the path of turning away from worldly activity; withdrawal. Literally, "to turn back." The path of renunciation.

Nivritti Marga: The path of renunciation or sannyasa, of withdrawal from the world.

Nivritti rupa: Of the very form of renunciation and detachment; Atman or Brahman.

Niyama: Observance; the five Do's of Yoga: 1) shaucha–purity, cleanliness; 2) santosha–contentment, peacefulness; 3) tapas–austerity, practical (i.e., result-producing) spiritual discipline; 4) swadhyaya–self-study, spiritual study; 5) Ishwarapranidhana–offering of one's life to God.

Niyamaka: He who controls; God or Ishvara.

Niyanta: Controller.

Nyasa: Renunciation; laying down.
Nyaya: Logic; one of the six schools of Indian philosophy.

O

Ojas: Vitality; vigor; luster; splendor; energy; spiritual energy. The highest form of energy in the human body. In the spiritual aspirant who constantly practices continence and purity, other forms of energy are transmuted into ojas and stored in the brain, manifesting as spiritual and intellectual power.

Om: The Pranava or the sacred syllable symbolizing and embodying Brahman.

Omkara: Om.

Om Tat Sat: A designation of Brahman; used as a benediction, a solemn invocation of the divine blessing.

P

Pada: Foot.
Pada Puja: Worship of the feet of a holy person.
Padma: Lotus.
Padmasana: Lotus posture; considered the best posture for meditation.
Panchabhuta: The Five Elements (Mahabhuta): ether (akasha), air (vayu), fire (agni), water (ap), and earth (prithvi).
Panchagni: "Five fires." A discipline in which four fires are kindled in the four cardinal directions and meditation is done from dawn till dusk seated in their midst, the sun being the fifth "fire." Also called Panchatapa.
Panchakshara: Mantra of Lord Shiva, consisting of five letters, viz., (Om) Na-mah-shi-va-ya.
Panchakosha: Five sheaths of ignorance enveloping the Self.
Panchanga: The traditional Indian (Hindu) calendar. "It provides precise information about astrological factors, planets, and stars which influence and alter the nature of the subtle environment" (*A Concise Dictionary of Indian Philosophy*).
Panchatapa: See Panchagni.

Pandal: A flat-roofed tent whose sides and top are detached from one another, the roof usually being higher than the sides to provide air circulation.

Pandavas: The five sons of King Pandu: Yudhishthira, Bhima, Arjuna, Nakula, and Sahadeva. Their lives are described in the Mahabharata.

Pandharpur: The major pilgrim city for Vaishnavas in Maharashtra, site of the famous Vithoba (or Vithala) Temple of Lord Krishna.

Pandit(a): Scholar; pundit; learned individual; a man of wisdom.

Panditya: Erudition; learning; intellectual Mastery.

Panduranga: Krishna, in the form worshipped in the Vithoba Temple in Pandharpur.

Papa(m): Sin; demerit; evil; sinful deeds; evil deeds; trouble; harm; anything which takes one away from dharma.

Papapurusha: Evil personified; personification of the sinful part of the individual.

Para(ma): Highest; universal; transcendent; supreme.

Parabhakti: Supreme devotion to God. This leads to jnana.

Parabrahman: Supreme Brahman.

Paraloka: The world beyond this world; the future life. Not a technical term for a particular level or loka, but just a general term for a/the world we go to after death.

Param[a]guru: The guru's guru.

Paramahan[m]sa/Paramhan[m]sa: Literally: Supreme Swan, a person of the highest spiritual realization, from the fact that a swan can separate milk from water and is therefore an apt symbol for one who has discarded the unreal for the Real, the darkness for the Light, and mortality for the Immortal, having separated himself fully from all that is not God and joined himself totally to the Divine, becoming a veritable embodiment of Divinity manifested in humanity.

Paramananda: Supreme (param) bliss (ananda).

Paramapada: The highest abode; the supreme abode (Vaikuntha) of Lord Vishnu.

Param[a]purusha: See Purusha.

Paramartha: The highest attainment, purpose, or goal; absolute truth; Reality.

Paramarthika (paramarthic): The Absolute; the absolutely real; in an absolute sense, as opposed to vyavaharika or relative.

Paramatma(n): The Supreme Self, God.

Parambrahma: The Supreme Absolute; the transcendental Reality.

Parameshthi: The exalted one; a name generally applied to Brahma or Hiranyagarbba, and sometimes even to Lord Narayana or the Supreme Purusha.

Parameshwara: The Supreme (Param) Lord (eshwara; Ishwara).

Paramhansa: See Paramahan[m]sa/Paramhan[m]sa above.

Paramhansa Yogananda: The most influential yogi of the twentieth century in the West, author of *Autobiography of a Yogi* and founder of Self-Realization Fellowship in America.

Paramjyotih: Supreme Light; Brahman.

Parampurusha: The Supreme Spirit; Supreme Person.

Paranirvana (Pali: Paranibbana): The Supreme, Final

Nirvana, when the perfectly enlightened individual is released from physical embodiment, never to return to birth in any world, high or low.

Parasamvit: Supreme knowledge; supreme consciousness; the supreme experiencing principle; absolute experience; self-luminous knowledge; pure consciousness; Shiva; Supreme Reality.

Parashakti: Supreme Power.

Paratpara: Greater than the great; higher than the high.

Paravairagya: Highest type of dispassion; the mind turns away completely from worldly objects and cannot be brought back to them under any circumstances.

Paravidya: Higher knowledge; direct knowledge of Brahman.

Paridrishtah: Regulated; measured; observed or viewed with the intent to regulate.

Parigraha: Possessiveness, greed, selfishness, acquisitiveness; covetousness; receiving of gifts conducive to luxury.

Parikrama: Circumambulation; "to traverse around." It is the custom in India to circumambulate sacred objects and places, always moving clockwise so the sacred thing or place is to the right of the devotee.

Parinama: Change; modification; transformation; evolution; development; effect; result; ripening; altering/changing.

Parinama-vada: The theory that the cause is continually transforming itself into its effects. The belief that Brahman transforms a portion of His Being into the universe. The belief that Prakriti is transformed into the world.

Paripurna: All-full; self-contained.

Parivrajaka: "One who wanders;" a roaming ascetic; one who has renounced the world; a sannyasin.

Parvati: "Daughter of the Mountain;" the daughter of King Himalaya; the consort of Shiva; an incarnation of the Divine Mother.

Pashupati: Lord of the individual souls (which are the Pashus or cattle); a name of Lord Shiva.

Pashyanti: The first prearticulated aspect of sound; sound in a subtle form as it starts to manifest before reaching the mind; the first perceptible form of sound.

Patala: Nether world; hell. In ancient Sanskrit texts the Western Hemisphere is called Patal Desh, the Underworld.

Patanjali: A yogi of ancient India, a Nath Yogi and the author of the Yoga Sutras.

Pati: "Lord;" God; Master; Shiva.

Pativrata: A chaste woman devoted to her husband.

Pativrata dharma: The rules of life of a chaste woman devoted to her husband.

Pavaka: Agni.

Phala: Flower; fruit; result or effect.

Pice: A monetary unit. There were sixty-four pice in the old rupee, but now there are one hundred.

Pinda (1): Part of the whole; individual; the body–either of the individual jiva or the cosmic body of Ishwara. It can also mean an organized whole or a unity of diversities.

Pinda (2): Small ball of rice offered to one's ancestors as an oblation. Sometimes in the sannyas ritual the prospective sannyasi performs his own funeral obsequies (shraddha ceremony), including making offerings of rice balls to/for himself.

Pindanda: The world of the body; microcosm as opposed to the macrocosm or cosmos.

Pindotpatti: The origin of the bodies, cosmic as well as individual.

Pingala: The subtle channel that extends from the base of the spine to the medulla on the right side of the spine.

Pipasa: Desire to drink; thirst.

Pishacha: A vampiristic spirit or demon, sometimes called "a blood drinker," though it really depletes its victims of prana, the life force.

Pitamaha: Grandfather; Great Father; titles of Brahma, the Creator.

Pitha: Seat; throne; chair. It also indicates a place where something is centered or established. For example, a place of power may be referred to as a "shakti pitha" or a place favorable to meditation as a "yoga pitha." A shrine to a deity may also be called a pitha, such as "Sarada pitha," etc., meaning that the deity resides or is established there.

Pitri: A departed ancestor, a forefather.

Pitriloka: The world occupied by the divine hierarchy of ancestors.

Prabha: Light; splendor; radiance.

Prabhu: Lord.

Prabodha: Awakening; becoming conscious; consciousness; manifestation; appearance; knowledge; understanding; intelligence.

Prabuddha: Awakened; conscious of the Ultimate Reality.

Pradakshina: Circumambulation of a sacred object or place, walking around it clockwise keeping it always on your right side.

Pradhana: Prakriti; causal matter.

Prahlada: A daitya prince who rejected his daitya heritage and became a devotee of Vishnu. His father, the evil Hiranyakashipu, tortured him and attempted his life because of his devotion and his speaking to others of divine matters, yet he remained steadfast.

Prajapati: Progenitor; the Creator; a title of Brahma the Creator.

Prajna: Consciousness; awareness; wisdom; intelligence.

Prajñanam Brahma: "Consciousness is Brahman." The Mahavakya (Great Saying) of the Aitareya Upanishad.

Prajnatma: The intelligent self; the conscious internal self.

Prakash(a): Shining; luminous; effulgence; illumination; luminosity; light; brightness. Pure Consciousness, from the root kash (to shine) and pra (forth); cognition.

Prakashaka: Revealer; illuminator.

Prakata: Manifest; revealed.

Prakritapralaya: Cosmic dissolution at the end of Hiranyagarbha's span of life, when He is liberated.

Prakriti: Causal matter; the fundamental power (shakti) of God from which the entire cosmos is formed; the root base of all elements; undifferentiated matter; the material cause of the world. Also known as Pradhana. Prakriti can also mean the entire range of vibratory existence (energy).

Prakritilaya: Absorbed or submerged in Prakriti; the state of yogis who have so identified with the cosmic energy that they are trapped in it as though in a net and cannot separate themselves from it and evolve onwards until the cosmic dissolution (pralaya) occurs in which the lower worlds of men, angels, and archangels (bhur, bhuwah and swar lokas) are dissolved.

Pralaya: Dissolution. See Mahapralaya.

Pramada: Carelessness; fault; guilt.

Pramana: Means of valid knowledge; logical proof; authority (of knowledge); means of cognition (from the verb root ma–to measure and pra–before or forward.

Pramanya: Truth; validity.

Pramata: Measurer; knower; the ego or the Jiva.

Prameya: Object of proof (Brahman or the Absolute Reality); subject of enquiry; object of right knowledge; measured or known object.

Pramoda: The pleasure which one gets through the actual enjoyment of an object; the third state of enjoyment of an object, after Priya and Moda, the attributes of the causal body.

Prana: Life; vital energy; life-breath; life-force; inhalation. In the human body the prana is divided into five forms: 1) Prana, the prana that moves upward; 2) Apana: The prana that moves downward, producing the excretory functions in general. 3) Vyana: The prana that holds prana and apana together and produces circulation in the body. 4) Samana: The prana that carries the grosser material of food to the apana and brings the subtler material to each limb; the general force of digestion. 5) Udana: The prana which brings up or carries down what has been drunk or eaten; the general force of assimilation.

Pranam: "To bow;" to greet with respect. A respectful or reverential gesture made by putting the hands together palm-to-palm in front of the chest. A prostration before a deity or revered person.

Pranamaya kosha: "The sheath of vital air (prana)." The sheath consisting of vital forces and the (psychic) nervous system, including the karmendriyas.

Pranapratishta: "Installation of life;" a ritual which is done to an image when it is set on the altar of a temple at its consecration. This ritual makes the image alive in a subtle–but no less real–sense.

Pranashakti: Subtle vital power.

Pranava: A title of Om, meaning "Life-ness" or "Life-Giver." Om is the expression or controller of prana–the life force within the individual being and the cosmos.

Pranavayu: The upward moving prana in the body, controller of the heart and lungs.

Pranayama: Control of the subtle life forces, often by means of special modes of breathing. Therefore breath control or breathing exercises are usually mistaken for pranayama. It also means the refining (making subtle) of the breath, and its lengthening through spontaneous slowing down of the respiratory rate.

Pranidhana: Self-surrender; prostration.

Prapancha: The world; appearance of the world.

Prarabdha: Karma that has become activated and begun to manifest and bear fruit in this life; karmic "seeds" that have begun to "sprout."

Prasad(am): Grace; food or any gift that has been first offered in worship or to a saint; that which is given by a saint. It also means tranquility, particularly in the Bhagavad Gita.

Prashanta: Calmed; quiet; tamed; intensified peace.

Prashanta-vahita: Continuity of a tranquil state of mind.

Pratibha: Special mental power; imaginative insight; intelligence; splendor of knowledge; intuition; ever-creative activity or consciousness; the spontaneous supreme "I"-consciousness; Parashakti.

Pratika: An image or symbol of God for worship and spiritual contemplation.

Pratima: Image; symbol; reflection; idol; figure; creator.

Pratipaksha bhavana(m): The method of substituting the opposite through imagination; thus, fear is overcome by dwelling strongly upon its opposite, viz., courage. Reflecting on and cultivating those traits which are opposed to spiritual obstructions.

Pratishta: Establishment; installation (see Pranapratishta); firm resting; reputation; fame. Gross matter; earth (from prati: "down upon" and stha: "to stand."

Pratiti: Perception; apprehension; insight; complete understanding; conviction; faith, confidence, belief, trust, credit; fame, respect; delight.

Pratyabhijna: Knowing; recognition or recovering

consciousness; recollection.

Pratyabhijnajnana: Same as pratyabhijna.

Pratyagatma: Inner Self; Katastha; Brahman.

Pratyahara: Abstraction or withdrawal of the senses from their objects, the fifth limb of Patanjali's Ashtanga Yoga.

Pratyaksha: Perception; direct perception; intuition.

Pratyakshapramana: Proof of direct perception or intuition.

Pratyaya: Cause; mental effort; imagination; idea of distinction.

Pratyayau: Content of the mind-field; presented idea; cognition principle; cognition; causal/awareness principle; awareness perceiving [through the mind]; buddhi; discriminatory intelligence; immediate arising thought directed to an object; cause; mental effort; imagination; idea of distinction.

Pravritta: One who follows the Pravritii Marga of active involvement in the world–attached action.

Pravritti: Action; endeavor. Literally: "to turn forth." Active involvement in the world; attached action.

Pravritti Marga: The path of active involvement in the world. The path of action or life in worldly society or according to the nature of the world.

Prayag: Rudraprayag, the modern-day Allahabad, site of the Triveni–the confluence of the three sacred rivers: Ganges, Jumna (Yamuna), and Saraswati.

Prayaschitta: Atonement (through various prescribed acts); expiation; mortification.

Prayascitta karma: Expiatory action; bodily mortification; penance.

Prayatna: Effort; attempt; conscious activity.

Prayojana: Result; fruit; the final end.

Prema: Love; divine love (for God).

Prema-bhakti: Intense love of God.

Premabhava: Feeling of love.

Premeshananda, Swami: Affectionately known as "Premesh Maharaj," Swami Premeshananda was a disciple of Sri Sri Ma Sarada Devi, the wife of Sri Ramakrishna Paramhansa, and a renowned monk of the Ramakrishna Order.

Prerana: Goading or stirring; impulse; urge; prompting.

Preta: Ghost; spirit of the dead.

Preyo marga: The path of the pleasing, the pleasant, the pleasurable, or of worldly gain, as opposed to the path of the good or truly beneficial.

Prithvi: The element of earth with density and fragrance as its characteristic features.

Prithivitattva: Principle of earth-element.

Priya(m): Dear; beloved; pleasing. It can also mean the happiness or joy felt when seeing a beloved object.

Puja: Worship; ceremonial (ritual) worship; adoration; honor. Usually involving the image of a deity.

Pujari: One who performs ritualistic worship (puja).

Punarjanma: "Birth again;" rebirth/reincarnation.

Pundit: Scholar; pandita; learned individual.

Punya: Merit; virtue; meritorious acts; virtuous deeds. See Apunya.

Punyamati: Virtuously inclined.

Puraka: Inhalation of breath.

Purana: Literally "The Ancient." The Puranas are a number of scriptures attributed to the sage Vyasa that teach spiritual principles and practices through stories about sacred historical personages which often include their teachings given in conversations.

Purana Purusha: The Ancient Person; God.

Purascharana: An observance consisting of the repetition of a mantra–as many hundred thousand times as there are "letters" (Sanskrit consonants) in it. This is done with rigid rules regarding diet, number of japa to be done per day, seat, etc.

Purna: Full; complete; infinite; absolute; Brahman.

Purnayogi: A full-blown Yogi.

Purnima: Full moon day.

Purohit: Priest; particularly a family priest.

Purusha: "Person" in the sense of a conscious spirit. Both God and the individual spirits are purushas, but God is the Adi (Original, Archetypal) Purusha, Parama (Highest) Purusha, and the Purushottama (Highest or Best of the Purushas).

Purushartha: The four goals (artha) of human life: wealth (artha), desire (kama), righteousness (dharma), and liberation (moksha). The first is the economic value, the second is the psychological value, the third is the moral value, and the fourth is the spiritual value. Human effort; individual exertion; right exertion.

Purushottama: The Supreme Person; Supreme Purusha; the Lord of the universe. (See Purusha.)

Purva karma: Previous karma; karma from the past, in this life or other life or lives.

Purva samskaras: Previous samskaras; that is, samskaras brought over from previous lives.

Purvashram: Previous stage of life.

Pushan: Surya, the Sun-god.

Pushpa: Flower.

Pushpaka: An ancient Indian flying machine.

Pushpanjali: Flower offering.

Putraishana: Desire for progeny.

R

Radha: The beloved of Sri Krishna during his early life in Brindaban; an incarnation of the divine feminine as Krishna is an incarnation of the divine masculine. Though her role (lila) was highly symbolic, nevertheless she was not a myth but a very real person. Furthermore, since she and Krishna were both children, their love for one another and their interaction was thoroughly spiritual and sacred. Any other depiction or interpretation is erroneous.

Raga: Blind love; attraction; attachment that binds the soul to the universe. Attachment/affinity for something, implying a desire for it. This can be emotional (instinctual) or intellectual. It may range from simple liking or preference to intense desire and attraction. Greed; passion. See Dwesha.

Raga-bhakti: Supreme love, making one attached only to God.

Raga-dwesha: The continual cycle of attraction and repulsion; like and dislike; love and hatred.

Raga-ragini: Melodic structures in music.

Raja: King.

Raja Yoga: See Ashtanga Yoga.

Rajarshi: "Royal sage;" a king who knows Brahman; an epithet of King Janaka.

Rajas: Activity, passion, desire for an object or goal.

Rajasa: See Rajasic.

Rajasahamkara: Egoism born of passion and activity.

Rajasic: Possessed of the qualities of the raja guna (rajas). Passionate; active; restless.

Rajkumar: Crown prince.

Rajoguna: Activity, passion, desire for an object or goal.

Raki: A (usually) red string tied around the right wrist–usually by a priest in a temple or holy place–as mantras are recited for blessing and protection.

Rakshasa: There are two kinds of rakshasas: 1) semidivine, benevolent beings, or 2) cannibal demons or goblins, enemies of the gods. Meat-eating human beings are sometimes classed as rakshasas.

Rakta: Blood; red; amoured; affected with love.

Ram: A title of Brahman the Absolute. Though sometimes used as a contraction of the name of Rama, many yogis insist that it is properly applied to Brahman alone and employ it as a mantra in repetition and meditation to reveal the Absolute. Interestingly, Ram (Rahm) is also a title of God in Hebrew.

Rama: An incarnation of God–the king of ancient Ayodhya in north-central India. His life is recorded in the ancient epic Ramayana.

Rama Nama: The name of Rama–both of the Absolute Brahman and of the incarnation, Rama of Ayodhya–used in devotional singing, japa and meditation.

Rama Tirtha (Swami): One of the key spiritual figures in late nineteenth and early twentieth century India. Born in Maharashtra, after being a university professor of mathematics in the Punjab for some years, he took sannyas and traveled throughout India and even to Japan and America in 1902, where he taught Indian philosophy and yoga (especially in San Francisco) for two years before returning to India.

Ramakrishna, Sri: Sri Ramakrishna lived in India in the second half of the nineteenth century, and is regarded by all India as a perfectly enlightened person–and by many as an Incarnation of God.

Ramana: Enjoyer; one who enjoys or delights in something.

Ramana Maharshi: A great twentieth-century sage from Tamil Nadu, who lived most of his life at or on the sacred mountain of Arunachala in the town of Tiruvannamalai.

Ramanuja (Sri): The great Vaishnava teacher of the eleventh century who formulated the philosophy known as Vishishtadvaita Vedanta (Qualified Non-Dualism).

Rama Tirtha (Swami): A renowned monk born in Maharashtra who came to America in 1902 and for two years taught philosophy and yoga, especially in San Francisco, before returning to India.

Ramayana: The great Sanskrit epic poem by the sage Valmiki describing the life of Rama, the king of ancient Ayodhya in north-central India, who is regarded as an incarnation of God. The renowned Hindi devotional poem by the saint

Tulsidas, also on the life of Rama.

Ramdas (Swami): One of the best-known and most influential spiritual figures of twentieth-century India, founder of Anandashram in South India and author of the spiritual classic *In the Vision of God* as well as many other inspirational books.

Ramnam: "The Name of Rama." Japa or kirtan of the Name, titles, or mantra(s) of Rama.

Rani: Queen.

Rasa: Taste; essence; savor; juice; nectar of delight.

Rasakrida: Transcendental sport that Lord Krishna played with the gopis and gopas of Brindaban.

Rasalila: See Rasakrida.

Ratna: Gem; jewel; the best.

Ravana: The demon king of Lanka, who kidnapped Sita and was subsequently slain by Rama.

Rechaka: Exhalation of breath.

Riddhi: Highest experiential delight; nine varieties of extraordinary exaltation and grandeur that come to a yogi as he advances and progresses in Yoga, like the supernatural powers or siddhis. Increase; growth; prosperity; success; wealth.

Rig Veda: The oldest scripture of India, considered the oldest scripture of the world, that consists of hymns revealed in meditation to the Vedic Rishis (seers). Although in modern times there are said to be four Vedas (Rig, Sama, Yajur, and Atharva), in actuality, there is only one Veda: the Rig Veda. The Sama Veda is only a collection of Rig Veda hymns that are marked (pointed) for singing. The Yajur Veda is a small book giving directions on just one form of Vedic sacrifice. The Atharva Veda is only a collection of theurgical mantras to be recited for the cure of various afflictions or to be recited over the herbs to be taken as medicine for those afflictions.

Rik (or Ric): A hymn, usually a hymn of the Rig Veda.

Rishabhadeva: An ancient ascetic who wandered freely through the forests, possessing nothing–not even wearing clothes–virtually unaware of his body.

Rishi: Sage; seer of the Truth.

Rita(m): Truth; Law; Right; Order. The natural order of things, or Cosmic Order/Law. Its root is ri, which means "to rise, to tend upward." It is said to be the basis for the Law of Karma.

Ritambharaprajna: Truth consciousness; consciousness that is full of truth.

Ruchi: Taste; appetite; liking; desire.

Rudra: Shiva. Derived from rud–he who drives away sin or suffering.

Rudras: "Roarers;" Vedic deities of destruction for renewal, the chief of which is Shiva; storm gods.

Rudraksha: "The Eye of Shiva;" a tree seed considered sacred to Shiva and worn by worshippers of Shiva, Shakti, and Ganesha, and by yogis, usually in a strand of 108 seeds. Also used as a rosary to count the number of mantras repeated in japa.

Rupa: Form; body.

S

Sabha: Assembly.

Sabija: "With seed;" with attributes; producing samskaras or subtle karmas.

Sabija samadhi: Savikalpa samadhi wherein the seeds of samskaras or karmas are not destroyed, and which produces the highest and subtlest of samskaras or karmas.

Sachchidananda: Existence-knowledge-bliss Absolute. (Also, Sat-cit-ananda.)

Sadachara: Morality; right behavior.

Sadagati: Everlasting happiness; final beatitude.

Sadashiva: Eternally auspicious; eternally happy; eternally prosperous. A title of Shiva, the eternally auspicious One.

Sad-darshanas: The six orthodox systems of Indian philosophy: Nyaya, Vaisheshika, Sankhya, Yoga, Mimamsa, and Vedanta.

Sadguru: True guru, or the guru who reveals the Real (Sat: God).

Sadhaka: One who practices spiritual discipline–sadhana–particularly meditation.

Sadhana: Spiritual practice.

Sadhana-chatushtaya: The fourfold aids to spiritual practice: 1) Viveka, the ability to discriminate between the transient and the eternal (nitya-anity-astu-viveka); 2) Vairagya, the absence of desire for securing pleasure or pain either here or elsewhere (iha-anutra-artha-phala-vairagya); 3) Shad-Sampat (The Sixfold Virtue): Sama, the serenity or tranquillity of mind which is brought about through the eradication of desires; Dama, the rational control of the senses; Uparati, satiety or resolutely turning the mind away from desire for sensual enjoyment; Titiksha, the power of endurance (an aspirant should patiently bear the pairs of opposites such as heat and cold, pleasure and pain, etc.; Shraddha, intense faith, lasting, perfect and unshakable; Samadhana, fixing the mind on Brahman or the Self, without allowing it to run towards objects; 4) Mumukshutwa, the intense desire for liberation.

Sadhana Shakti: Both the power to successfully engage in sadhana, the the power that accrues within the sadhaka from his practice of sadhana.

Sadhu (1): Seeker for truth (sat); a person who is practicing spiritual disciplines; a good or virtuous or honest man, a holy man, saint, sage, seer. Usually this term is applied only to monastics.

Sadhu (2): Straight; right; leading straight to a goal; hitting the mark; unerring; straightened; not entangled; well-disposed; kind willing; obedient; successful; effective; ready; prepared; peaceful; powerful; fit; proper; right; good;

virtuous; honorable; righteous; well-born; noble; correct; pure; excellent; perfect.

Sadhvi: A female "sadhu."

Sadvichara: Right enquiry; enquiry into Truth.

Sadyomukti: Immediate liberation.

Sadhyas: A group of celestial beings with exquisitely refined natures thought to inhabit the ether.

Sagar[a]: Ocean; sea.

Saguna: Possessing attributes or qualities (gunas).

Saguna Brahman: Brahman with attributes, such as mercy, omnipotence, omniscience, etc.; the Absolute conceived as the Creator, Preserver, and Destroyer of the universe; also the Personal God according to the Vedanta.

Sahaja: Natural; innate; spontaneous; inborn.

Sahaja Nirvikalpa Samadhi: Natural, non-dual state of Brahmic Consciousness.

Sahaja samadhi: See Sahaja Nirvikalpa Samadhi.

Sahajanishtha: Natural and normal establishment; establishment in one's own essential nature of Satcidananda.

Sahajavastha: Superconscious state that has become natural and continuous.

Sahasrara: The "thousand-petalled lotus" of the brain. The highest center of consciousness, the point at which the spirit (atma) and the bodies (koshas) are integrated and from which they are disengaged.

Sahasr(ar)adala: The Sahasrara chakra located in the center of the brain according to the Nath Panth tradition.

Sai Baba: See Shirdi Sai Baba.

Sakama: Action with expectation of fruits.
Sakara: With form.
Sakhya: The attitude of a devotee, expressing the relationship of a friend with God; examples are Arjuna, Uddhava and the cowherds of Brindavana.
Sakshatakara: Self-realization; direct experience; experience of Absoluteness; Brahmajnana.
Sakshi(n): a witness; the Witness Self; the kutashtha which passively observes the actions of the body and the senses; seer; the intuitive faculty.
Sakshiavastha: Permanent establishment in the Witness State.
Sakshibhava: The attitude of remaining as a witness.
Sakshichaitanya: Witnessing intelligence or consciousness.
Sakshichetana: Witnessing soul; Kutastha; same as Sakshicaitanya.
Sakshidrashta: Witnessing subject; witnessing seer.
Sakshitwa: Establishment in the consciousness of being the Witness Self; looking upon oneself as merely the observer.
Salokya: Being in the same plane or world as God.
Sama: Calmness; tranquillity; control of the internal sense organs; control of mind; calmness of mind; the state in which the mind is kept in the heart and not allowed to externalize; it is the constant eradication of the mental tendencies, according to the *Aparoksha Anubhuti* of Shankara; same; equal.
Sama Veda: A collection of Rig Veda hymns that are marked (pointed) for singing. It is sometimes spoken of as the "essence" of the Rig Veda.

Samabbavana: Feeling of equality.

Samadhana: Equal fixing; proper concentration.

Samadarshana: Equal vision; seeing all things equally; equal-sightedness; equanimity.

Samadhana: Equal fixing; proper concentration; complete concentration; the root word of samadhi.

Samadhi: The state of superconsciousness where Absoluteness is experienced attended with all-knowledge and joy; Oneness; here the mind becomes identified with the object of meditation; the meditator and the meditated, thinker and thought become one in perfect absorption of the mind. See Samprajñata Samadhi, Asamprajñata Samadhi, Savikalpa Samadhi, and Nirvikalpa Samadhi.

Samadrishti: See Samadarshana.

Samana: The prana the carries the grosser material of food to the apana and brings the subtler material to each limb; the general force of digestion.

Samarasya: Homogeneity; oneness–especially of essence–which results from the elimination of all differences; equilibrium; the process of bringing the body into a harmonious resonance with the Divine.

Samarth Ramdas: A renowned saint and poet of Maharastra; guru of the great warrior-king Shivaji; rishi of the mantra: Sri Ram Jai Ram Jai Jai Ram.

Samasti: Cosmic; collective; an integrated whole of the same class of entity.

Samata: Balanced state of mind.

Samatva: Equanimity (under all conditions); equanimity of outlook (making no distinction between friend and foe, pleasure and pain, etc.)

Samavaya: Combination; union; conjunction; constant and inseparable connection or inherence; existence of one thing in another.

Sambandha: Relationship; connection.

Samhara: Destruction.

Samhita: A division of the Vedas; Vedic hymns.

Samjnana: Consciousness; sentience.

Sampat: Perfection; wealth; virtue.

Sampatti: Same as Sampat.

Sampradaya: Tradition; philosophical school; literally: "handed-down instruction;" also a line of initiatic empowerment.

Samprajnata: A stage in samadhi wherein one is conscious of an object; that mind functions in this stage and concentrates on an object of knowledge (perception).

Samprajñata samadhi: State of superconsciousness, with the triad of meditator, meditation and the meditated; lesser samadhi; cognitive samadhi; samadhi of wisdom; meditation with limited external awareness. Savikalpa samadhi.

Samprasada: Peace; serenity; calmness; tranquillity.

Samprayoga: Contact of the senses with their objects; communication; interchange; uniting; connecting.

Samsara: Life through repeated births and deaths; the wheel of birth and death; the process of earthly life.

Samsara chakra: The wheel of birth and death.

Samsari: The transmigrating soul.

Samsaric: Having to do with samsara; involved with samsara;

partaking of the traits or qualities of samsara.

Samsarin: One who is subject to samsara–repeated births and deaths–and who is deluded by its appearances, immersed in ignorance.

Samshaya: Doubt; suspicion.

Samshayabhavana: Feeling of doubt or suspicion.

Samskara (1): Impression in the mind, either conscious or subconscious, produced by action or experience in this or previous lives; propensities of the mental residue of impressions; subliminal activators; prenatal tendency. See Vasana.

Samskara (2): A ritual that makes an impression or change in the individual for whom it is done. There are sixteen samskaras prescribed by the dharma shastras, beginning with conception (garbhadan) and concluding with the rite for the departed soul (antyshthi). The major ones besides these two are the birth rite (jatakarman), naming ceremony (namakaranam), the first eating of solid food (annaprasannam), the first cutting of the hair (chudakaraman), bestowal of the sacred thread and instruction in the Gayatri mantra (upanayanam), marriage (vivahanam), taking up of the retired life (vanaprastha), and taking up the monastic life (sannyasa). They are all done at points in the person's life when significant changes in the subtle energy bodies are going to take place. Thus the samskara protects and strengthens the individual at those times and also prepares him for those changes, making actual alterations in his subtle bodies. Although they are often made social occasions, they are very real instruments of change to facilitate and further the person's personal evolution. They are the linchpins of dharmic life, and essentially spiritual events.

Samskaraskandha: The group of old impressions.

Samsriti: World-process; same as Samsara.

Samvega: Intense ardor derived from long practice.

Samvit: Knowledge; consciousness; awareness; intelligence; supreme consciousness.

Samyama: Self-control; perfect restraint; an all-complete condition of balance and repose. The combined practice of the last three steps in Patanjali's Ashtanga Yoga: concentration (dharana), meditation (dhyana), and union (samadhi). See the Vibhuti Pada of the Yoga Sutras.

Samyavastha: State of equilibrium; harmony of the three gunas; the state of the unmanifested being.

Samyoga: Conjunction; contact.

Samyukta: United; combined.

Sanaka: One of the Four Kumaras (see Kumaras).

Sananda: With bliss (a kind of Samadhi).

Sanandana: One of the Four Kumaras (see Kumaras).

Sanatana: Eternal; everlasting; ancient; primeval.

Sanatana Dharma: "The Eternal Religion," also known as "Arya Dharma," "the religion of those who strive upward [Aryas]." Hinduism.

Sanatana Dharmi: One who follows Sanatana Dharma.

Sanatkumara: One of the Four Kumaras (see Kumaras).

Sanatkumaras: The Four Kumaras (see Kumaras).

Sanatsujata: One of the Four Kumaras (see Kumaras).

Sancharana: Movement.

Sanchita: Sanchita karma.

Sanchita karma: The vast store of accumulated actions done in the past, the fruits of which have not yet been reaped.

Sandhya: A ritual done at the "junctions" (sandhyas) of the day–dawn, noon, and sunset–during which the Savitri Gayatri is repeated.

Sandhyavandana: A religious ablution and prayer among the twice-born of the Hindus performed in the morning, noon and evening.

Sang(h)a: Attachment; affinity; company; association; collection; community.

Sankalpa: A life-changing wish, desire, volition, resolution, will, determination, or intention–not a mere momentary aspiration, but an empowering act of will that persists until the intention is fully realized. It is an act of spiritual, divine creative will inherent in each person as a power of the Atma.

Sankhya: One of the six orthodox systems of Hindu philosophy whose originator was the sage Kapila, Sankhya is the original Vedic philosophy, endorsed by Krishna in the Bhagavad Gita (Gita 2:39; 3:3, 5; 18:13, 19), the second chapter of which is entitled "Sankhya Yoga." *A Ramakrishna-Vedanta Wordbook* says: "Sankhya postulates two ultimate realities, Purusha and Prakriti. Declaring that the cause of suffering is man's identification of Purusha with Prakriti and its products, Sankhya teaches that liberation and true knowledge are attained in the supreme consciousness, where such identification ceases and Purusha is realized as existing independently in its transcendental nature." Not surprisingly, then, Yoga is based on the Sankhya philosophy.

Sankhyabhih: Numbers.

Sankirtan: Singing the names and praises of God; devotional chanting.

Sannyas(a): Renunciation; monastic life. Sannyasa literally means "total throwing away," in the sense of absolute rejection of worldly life, ways and attitudes. True sannyas is based on viveka and vairagya. It is not just a mode of external life, but a profound insight and indifference to the things of the world and the world itself–not the world of God's creation, but the world of human ignorance, illusion, folly and suffering which binds all sentient beings to the wheel of continual birth and death. The sannyasi's one goal is liberation through total purification and enlightenment. His creed is Shankara's renowned Vedanta in Half a Verse: "Brahman is real. The world is illusion. The jiva is none other than Brahman."

Sannyasi(n): A renunciate; a monk.

Sannyasic: Pertaining to sannyasa and the life and thought of a sannyansin.

Sannyasini: A female renunciate; a nun.

Sanskrit: The language of the ancient sages of India and therefore of the Indian scriptures and yoga treatises.

Santosha: Contentment; joy; happiness; peacefulness.

Sapta Rishis: "Seven Sages." Great Beings who exist at the top of creation and supervise it.

Sarada Devi ("Holy Mother"): The virgin-wife of Sri Ramakrishna, and a great teacher in her own right, considered by many to be an incarnation of the Mother aspect of God.

Saraswati: The goddess of speech, wisdom, learning and the arts–particularly music.

Sarva(m): All; everything; complete.

Sarvajña(twa): Knowing everything; omniscience.

Sarvesha(m): All; everything; complete.

Sarupya: Having the same form as God.

Sarva: All; everything.

Sarvabhokta: All-enjoyer; an epithet of the Supreme Lord.

Sarvadeshika: Pertaining to all places; present everywhere.

Sarvagata: Present in all (things); omnipresent.

Sarvajna: Omniscient; knowing everything.

Sarvakalyana: All auspicious qualities.

Sarvakarana: Cause of everything; causality of creation, preservation and destruction.

Sarvakarita: All-doer; doer of everything.

Sarvantaryami: The Inner Ruler of everything.

Sarvasakshi: Witness of everything.

Sarvatmakatva: Universality; the state of being the soul of everything.

Sarvatva: State of being everything.

Sarvavit: All-knowing.

Sarvavyapi: All-pervading; omnipresent.

Sarveshwaratwa: Supreme rulership over all.

Sasmita: With the feeling of individuality or the egoistic feeling of "I exist"(a kind of Samadhi).

Sat: Existence; reality; truth; being; a title of Brahman, the Absolute or Pure Being.

Sat Chakras: The six chakras: Muladhara, Swadhishthana, Manipura, Anahata, Vishuddha and Ajna, located at the base of the spine, in the spine a little less than midway between the base of the spine and the area opposite the navel in the spine, the point in the spine opposite the navel, the point in the spine opposite the midpoint of the sternum bone, the point in the spine opposite the hollow of the throat, and the point between the eyebrows, respectively.

Satchidananda: Existence-Knowledge-Bliss Absolute; Brahman.

Satkama: Pure desire (of a liberated sage); desire for Moksha.

Satkarma: Righteous action.

Satkaryavada: The doctrine which holds that the effect is inherent in the cause and that the effect is only a change of the cause–that the effect exists prior to its manifestation in a latent state in the cause. This is a tenet of both Sankhya and Shaiva Siddhanta.

Satsang(a): Literally: "company with Truth." Association with godly-minded persons. The company of saints and devotees.

Satsankalpa: True resolve; pure desire; perfect will.

Sattwa: Light; purity; harmony, goodness, reality.

Sattwa Guna: Quality of light, purity, harmony, and goodness.

Sattwasamshuddhi: Purity of heart; purity of feeling; increase of light and purity.

Sattwic: Partaking of the quality of Sattwa.

Satya(m): Truth; the Real; Brahman, or the Absolute; truthfulness; honesty.

Satya Loka: "True World," "World of the True [Sat]", or "World of Truth [Satya]." This highest realm of relative existence where liberated beings live who have not entered back into the Transcendent Absolute where there are no "worlds" (lokas). From that world they can descend and return to other worlds for the spiritual welfare of others, as can those that have chosen to return to the Transcendent.

Satya Yuga: See Yuga.

Satyakama: He who longs or desires for Truth.

Satyasankalpa: Pure will.

Satyatwa: State of Truth.

Savichara: With deliberation and reasoning or enquiry.

Savichara samadhi: A stage in samadhi wherein the mind (chittta) is identified with some subtle object and assumes its form, being aware of what it is and capable of analyzing it by means of the purified buddhi; with deliberation and reasoning or inquiry.

Savikalpa: With doubt and change.

Savikalpa Samadhi: Samadhi in which there is objective experience or experience of "qualities" and with the triad of knower, knowledge and known; lesser samadhi; cognitive samadhi; samadhi of wisdom; meditation with limited external awareness. Samprajñata samadhi.

Savishesha Brahman: Brahman with attributes; Saguna Brahman.

Savitarka: With logic and argumentation.

Savitarka Samadhi: The union (samadhi) in which the mind concentrates on objects, remembering their names and qualities. (See Vitarka.)

Savitri: The sun; a title of Shiva; a title of Indra.

Savitri Gayatri: A mantra of the Rig Veda which is recited for unfoldment of the intellectual powers leading to enlightenment.

Sayujya: Closely united with; united with God; becoming one with God.

Sayujyata: The state of being in Sayujya.

Seva: Service; selfless service.

Sevak: Servant.

Shabda: Sound; word.

Shabda Brahman: Sound-God; Brahman in the Form of Sound; Omkara; the Vedas.

Shabda tanmatra: Subtle principle of sound.

Shabdakshara: "Sound-syllable;" Om.

Shadripu: The six enemies to realization of the Self: desire (kama), anger (krodha), greed (lobha), arrogance (mada), delusive attachment (moha) and jealousy (matsarya).

Shad-Sampat: The sixfold virtue: 1) Sama: serenity or tranquillity of mind which is brought about through the eradication of desires; 2) Dama: rational control of the senses; 3) Uparati: satiety–resolutely turning the mind away from desire for sensual enjoyment; 4) Titiksha: the power of endurance. An aspirant should patiently bear the pairs of opposites such as heat and cold, pleasure and pain, etc.; 5) Shraddha: intense faith, lasting, perfect and unshakable;

6) Samadhana: fixing the mind on Brahman or the Self, without allowing it to run towards objects.

Shaiva/Shaivite: A worshipper of Shiva; pertaining to Shiva.

Shakta: A worshipper of Shakti, the Divine Feminine.

Shakti: Power; energy; force; the Divine Power of becoming; the apparent dynamic aspect of Eternal Being; the Absolute Power or Cosmic Energy; the Divine Feminine.

Shaktipata: Descent of power (through Upasana).

Shama: Tranquillity; control of mind; calmness of mind; the mind is kept in the heart and not allowed to externalise; it is the constant eradication of the mental tendencies, according to Aparoksha Anubhati of Shankara.

Shambbavi mudra: The vacant externalised gaze of a Hatha Yogi where the mind is directed inwards; the Yogi appears to be looking at external objects but is not actually perceiving them as his mind is indrawn.

Shankara (1): "The Auspicious One." A title of Shiva.

Shankara (2): Shankaracharya; Adi (the first) Shankaracharya: The great reformer and re-establisher of Vedic Religion in India around 500 B.C. He is the unparalleled exponent of Advaita (Non-Dual) Vedanta. He also reformed the mode of monastic life and founded (or regenerated) the ancient Swami Order.

Shalagrama: A flat-round or disk-like stone with rounded edges, found only in the Mandakini River in the region of Tibet, considered to be a manifestation of Vishnu and His avataras.

Shama: Calmness; tranquility; control of the internal sense organs; same; equal.

Shanta: Peaceful; calm; tranquil; one who possesses shanti.

Shantam, Shivam, Advaitam: "Peaceful, Blissful, Non-Dual"– the definition of Brahman and the Self found in the seventh verse of the Mandukya Upanishad.

Shanti: Peace; calm; tranquility; contentment.

Shantirupa: Of the form of peace.

Sharanagati: One who has taken refuge or shelter, or sought protection.

Sharanam: Refuge; protection, shelter.

Sharira: Body; sheath; literally: "that which perishes," from the root shri which means "to waste away."

Shashvatapada: Everlasting abode.

Shastra: Scripture; spiritual treatise.

Shastri: One who is a scholar and teacher of the scriptures (shastras).

Shastric: Scriptural or having to do with the scriptures.

Shaucha: Purity; cleanliness.

Shesha: The endless; the infinite; The name of the snake (naga) upon which Vishnu reclines.

Shesha Narayana: The form of Vishnu reclining upon Shesha, the infinite (endless) snake (naga).

Shikha: A tuft of hair on the crown of the head, usually worn only by Brahmins or brahmacharis, but in the villages of Northern India many men of other castes wear the shikha as a sign that they are Hindus.

Shila (1): Conduct; good behavior; right discipline; morality; quality or property.

Shila (2): Stone; rock.

Shirdi Sai Baba: Perhaps the most renowned spiritual teacher of the nineteenth and twentieth centuries in India. His fame continues to grow in this century as well.

Shirsasana (or shirasana): the head stand of the Hatha Yogins.

Shirovratam: "Vow of the head; a vow in which fire is carried on the head or in which the head is shaven; sannyasa.

Shishya: Disciple; student.

Shiva: A name of God meaning "One Who is all Bliss and the giver of happiness to all." Although classically applied to the Absolute Brahman, Shiva can also refer to God (Ishwara) in His aspect of Dissolver and Liberator (often mistakenly thought of as "destroyer").

Shiva Linga: A column-like or egg-shaped symbol of Shiva, usually made of stone. The column-like linga represents the central axis of creation which was seen by Brahma and Vishnu as a column of Light that had no top or bottom, but out of which Shiva emerged and explained that he was the source–indeed the totality–of creation. To yogis it represents the sushumna nadi which embodies the Consciousness that is Shiva. The egg-shaped (garbha) linga represents Shiva as the germ or seed of the universe out of whom all things have come to be as his manifestation. It is often to considered to represent the universe itself which is identical with Shiva.

Shivapada: The state of Lord Shiva; blessedness.

Shivatma: The Paramatman who is the root cause of all the activities in the Universe.

Shivoham: I am Shiva.
Shodhana: Process of cleansing (purifying) in Hatha Yoga.
Shoka: Sorrow; grief.
Shraddha (1): Faith; confidence or assurance that arises from personal experience.
Shraddha (2): Rituals for the welfare of the dead, done in the days after the death and then usually done on the anniversary of the death.
Shrauta: Pertaining to or enjoined by the Shruti.
Shravana: Hearing; study; listening to reading of the scriptures or instruction in spiritual life.
Shreyas: Good; blessedness; Moksha.
Shri: Goddess Lakshmi; wealth; prosperity.
Shrotra: Ear; the sense or faculty of hearing.
Shruti: That which is heard; revealed scripture in the sense of divine communication. Usually applied to the Vedas, Shankara also spoke of the Upanishads as Shruti.
Shubha: Auspicious; blessed; fortunate.
Shuchi: Pure; untainted.
Shuddha: Pure; clear; clean; untainted.
Shuddha-chaitanya: Pure intelligence; pure consciousness.
Shuddhi: The state of purity (shuddha); purification.
Shudra: A member of the laborer, servant caste.
Shukla: White; bright.
Shukla sannyasa: "White sannyasa." The adoption of monastic life spontaneously, solely from a profound urge from within, without any formal external ritual or conferring of sannyasa by another person.

Shukra: Bright; resplendent; clear; pure; spotless; white; juice; the essence of anything; semen.

Shukracharya: The guru of the demons (asuras).

Shunya: Void; no-thing; emptiness.

Shvasa-prashvasa: Hard breathing; inspiration and expiration.

Shyama Charan Lahiri: See Lahiri Mahasaya.

Siddha: A perfected–liberated–being, an adept, a seer, a perfect yogi.

Siddha Nama: The Perfect Name; an title of the Soham Mantra.

Siddha Purusha: A perfectly enlightened being.

Siddhaloka: The highest realm of existence in which the fully liberated (siddhas) live. (However, wherever a siddha is, that place is siddhaloka.)

Siddhanta: Established tenet or doctrine.

Siddharudha: One who is established in the state of siddhi–spiritual perfection.

Siddhasana: A meditation posture.

Siddhi: Spiritual perfection; psychic power; power; modes of success; attainment; accomplishment; achievement; mastery; supernatural power attained through mantra, meditation, or other yogic practices. From the verb root sidh–to attain.

Sita: The consort of Rama, an avatara of the Divine Mother aspect of God.

Sivananda (Swami): A great twentieth-century Master, founder of the world-wide Divine Life Society, whose books on spiritual life and religion are widely circulated in the West as well as in India.

Skanda (1): Aggregate; a component of which human beings are comprised, five in number.

Skanda (2): See Subramunya.

Sloka: A Sanskrit verse. Usually it consists of two lines of sixteen syllables each, or four lines of eight syllables each.

Smarana: Remembrance (of God).

Smarta: Pertaining to or enjoined by the Smrti.

Smriti: Memory; recollection; "that which is remembered;" code of law. In this latter sense, Smriti is used to designate all scriptures except the Vedas and Upanishads (which are considered of greater authority: Shruti).

Sneha: Adhesiveness; friendship.

Soham: "That am I;" the ultimate Atma mantra, the mantra of the Self; the Ajapa Gayatri formula of meditation in which "So" is intoned mentally during natural inhalation and "Ham" is intoned mentally during natural exhalation. Soham is pronounced "Sohum," as the short "a" in Sanskrit is pronounced like the American "u" in "up."

Soham Bhava: The state of being and awareness: "THAT I am." Gorakhnath says that So'ham Bhava includes total Self-comprehension (ahamta), total Self-mastery (akhanda aishwarya), unbroken awareness of the unity of the Self (swatmata), awareness of the unity of the Self with all phenomenal existence–as the Self (vishwanubhava), knowledge of all within and without the Self–united in the Self (sarvajñatwa).

Soma: A milkweed, *Ascelpias acida*, whose juice in Vedic times was made into a beverage and offered in sacrifices; the nectar of immorality; a name of Chandra, the presiding deity of the moon.

Soshana: Emaciation; drying.

Spanda: Vibration; expanding vibration; flutter; throb; movement; creative shakti; movement; pulsation; creative pulsation; apparent motion in the motionless Shiva which brings about the manifestation, maintenance, and withdrawal of the universe; the principle of apparent movement from the state of absolute unity to the plurality of the world.

Sparsha: Touch; sense contact.

Sparshana: Touching.

Sphatika: Clear quartz crystal.

Sphota: The Sanskrit original of our English word "spot;" manifester; the idea which bursts or flashes–including the Pranava which burst or flashes forth from the Absolute and becomes transformed into the Relative.

Sphurana: Vibration.

Spriha: Desire; hankering,

Sreyo marga: The path of the good or truly beneficial, as opposed to the path of the merely appealing, pleasant, pleasurable, or that which leads to worldly gain.

Sri: Holy; sacred; excellent; venerated (venerable); revered; a term of respect similar to "Reverend." Also: prosperity, glory, and success–and therefore an epithet for Lakshmi, the goddess of wealth and abundance, the consort of Vishnu. It is often used as an honorific prefix to the name of deities and holy persons to indicate holiness (Sri Krishna, Sri

Swami N., etc.). Also used as the equivalent of the English "Mr." (Srimati would be the equivalent of "Mrs.")

Sri Vaishnava: A worshipper of Vishnu according to the philosophical school of Sri Ramanuja known as Vishishtadvaita Vedanta (Qualified Non-Dualism).

Sri Yantra: The mystical diagram showing the movement of the spiritual energies inherent in and produced by the mantra Om. The Sri Yantra has also come to be identified with the energy-power of the Divine Mother, and if often worshipped by her devotees.

Sri Yukteswar Giri, Swami: The guru of Paramhansa Yogananda.

Srimad Bhagavatam: One of the eighteen scriptures known as Puranas which are attributed to Vyasa.

Srishti: Creation; projection or gradual unfoldment of what exists potentially in the cause; evolution of the universe from its seed state.

Sruti: See Shruti.

Stambha: Suspended; retention; stationary; fixed; to fix firmly; support; sustain; prop; pillar.

Stambhana: Arresting; stopping; stupefaction.

Sthala: Abode; place; hall.

Sthana: Position; abode; residence.

Sthanumanushya: Man in the post; a simile used to describe false superimposition due to wrong imagination.

Sthavara: Immovable; immobile; stationary.

Sthira(m): Fixed; firm; still; steady; stable; enduring.

Sthirata (Sthirattwa): Steadiness or firmness of body or mind; the steady tranquillity born of meditation.

Sthitaprajna: One who is established in the divine Consciousness or superconsciousness.

Sthiti: Steadiness; condition or state; existence; being; subsistence; preservation.

Sthula: Gross material; physical entity; atomic matter.

Sthula samadhi: The state of samadhi which is of a Jada type in which there is no intuitive awareness.

Sthula sharira: Gross body; physical body; body of atomic matter.

Stotra: A hymn or verse in praise of God.

Stuti: Praise; glorification.

Styana: Dullness; languor, debility; drooping state.

Subramanya: The god of war and son of Shiva and Parvati; Skanda.

Sudarshana: Sudarshana Chakra.

Sudarshana Chakra: The invincible weapon of Lord Vishnu which is able to cut through anything, and is a symbol of the Lord's power of cutting through all things which bind the jiva to samsara. Thus it is the divine power of liberation (moksha).

Sukarma: Good action; good deed; virtuous; diligent.

Sukha(m): Happiness; ease; joy; happy; pleasure; pleasant; agreeable.

Sukhacintana: Thought of happiness; happy thinking.

Sukhadeva: The son of Vyasa who was liberated before coming into incarnation. He is considered a supreme renunciate, a perfect avadhuta.

Sukhi: One who is happy.

Sukrita: Good act; merit.

Sukshma: Fine; subtle; invisible; belonging to a subtler order of existence than the physical.

Sukshma sharira: Subtle body; astral body (also called linga sharira).

Sundara: Beautiful.

Sura: Divine being; deva; one who is filled with light.

Surya: The sun; the presiding deity of the sun, sometimes identified with Vishnu (Surya-Narayana) or the Absolute Brahman.

Surya nadi: Another name for the psychic nerve, Pingala.

Surya-mandala: The circle (orbit) of the sun.

Suryanarayana: God (Narayana) in the form of the Sun (Surya).

Sushila: He whose nature is purified, i.e., the man who regularly practises Yama and so forth and has trained himself.

Sushumna: A subtle passage in the midst of the spinal column, corresponding to the spinal cord, that extends from the base of the spine to the medulla oblongata in the head.

Sushupti: The dreamless sleep state.

Sutra: Literally: a thread; an aphorism with minimum words and maximum sense; a terse sentence; in Buddhism, an entire scripture.

Sutradhara: The holder of the string; Ishwara, the Lord of the universe.

Sutratma: "The thread-Self;" immanent deity of the totality of the subtle bodies, referring to the Gita verse: "Sutratma: "The thread-Self;" immanent deity of the totality of the subtle bodies, referring to the Gita verse: "All this creation is strung on me like pearls on a thread" (7:7).

Suvichara: Right enquiry.

Svara: Sound; accent; tone.

Swabhava: One's own inherent disposition, nature, or potentiality; inherent state of mind; state of inner being.

Swadharma: One's own natural (innate) duty (dharma, based on their karma and samskara. One's own prescribed duty in life according to the eternal law (ritam).

Swadhishthana chakra: Energy center located in the spine a little less than midway between the base of the spine and the area opposite the navel. Seat of the Water element.

Swadhyaya: Introspective self-study or self-analysis leading to self-understanding. Study of spiritual texts regarding the Self.

Swaha: An oblation or offering made to gods; an exclamation used in offering oblations to gods.

Swakarma: Action, duty, business or occupation determined by (according to) one's own innate nature.

Swami: Literally, "I am mine"–in the sense of absolute self-mastership. It could be legitimately translated: "He who is one with his Self [Swa]." It is often used in the sense of "lord" or owner as well as a spiritual guide or authority. God Himself is the ultimate Swami. As a matter of respect it is always used in reference to sannyasis, since they have vowed themselves to pursue the knowledge of the Self, or those considered to be of spiritual advancement.

Swami Maharaj of Akalkot (Swāmi Samarth Mahāraj;

Akkalkot Swami): A nineteenth century guru of the Dattatreya tradition (sampradaya), widely respected in the Indian states of Maharashtra, Karnataka and Andhra Pradesh. He lived in the Akkalkot village in Maharashtra for about twenty-two years.

Swanubhati: Direct experience of one's own Self.

Swapna: The dream state; a dream.

Swapna samadhi: Samadhi that occurs in a dream–that is, the dream passes into a superconscious state.

Swaprakasha: Self-luminous.

Swara: Sound; accent; tone.

Swarajya: "Self-rule;" independence; freedom; absolute freedom.

Swarga: Heaven-world; the celestial region.

Swarga loka: Swarga.

Swarupa: "Form of the Self." Natural–true–form; actual or essential nature; essence. A revelatory appearance that makes clear the true nature of some thing.

Swarupajnana: Knowledge which is of the nature of the Self; knowledge of one's essential nature; knowledge of pure consciousness, which is the highest end in life.

Swasa: Breath.

Swastika: "Sign of Auspiciousness;" a mark made on something to invoke good luck.

Swatantra: "Self-rule;" independence; freedom; absolute freedom; independent; free.

Swatantratva: State of (Absolute) independence.

Swayambhava: Feeling of independence.

Swayambhu: Self-existent or self-generated.
Swayamjyotih: Self-illumined; self-luminous.
Swayamprakash(a): Self-luminous; self-illumined.

T

Taijasa: The dream self; the vital self; the "fiery."

Taimni, I. K.: A professor of chemistry in India. He wrote many excellent books on philosophy and spiritual practice, including The Science of Yoga, a commentary on the Yoga Sutras. For many years he was the spiritual head of the Esoteric Section of the Theosophical Society headquartered in Adyar, Madras (Tamilnadu), and traveled the world without publicity or notoriety, quietly instructing many sincere aspirants in the path to supreme consciousness.

Talu chakra: Energy center located at the root of the palate opposite the tip of the nose.

Tamas: Dullness, darkness, inertia, folly, and ignorance.

Tamasic: Possessed of the qualities of the tamo guna (tamas). Ignorant; dull; inert; and dark.

Tandava: Dance of Destruction (Dissolution of the Cosmos) of Lord Shiva.

Tandra: Drowsiness; half-sleep state; an obstacle in meditation.

Tanha: Craving; desire; thirst.

Tanmatras: The pure elements; the subtle essence of the five elements, elemental essence.

Tantra: A manual of, or a particular path of, sadhana laying great stress upon japa of a mantra and other esoteric practices relating to the powers latent in the human complex of physical, astral, and causal bodies in relation to the cosmic Power usually thought as the Divine Feminine.

Tantrika: Pertaining to Tantra.

Tanumanasa: Threadlike (extremely subtle and attenuated) state of mind, indicating that impurities and impediments are lessening.

Tapa: Trouble; acute anxiety; anguish; suffering.

Tapa Loka: The world of tapasya; the world beyond rebirth where adept yogis perpetually engage in tapasya (yoga) until they attain liberation and pass upward into Satya Loka, the realm of the liberated ones who know Brahman.

Tapana: Burning; inflaming.

Tapas: See tapasya.

Tapasya: Austerity; practical (i.e., result-producing) spiritual discipline; spiritual force. Literally it means the generation of heat or energy, but is always used in a symbolic manner, referring to spiritual practice and its effect, especially the roasting of karmic seeds, the burning up of karma.

Tapaswi(n): Ascetic; one who is practising Tapas.

Tapatraya: Sufferings or afflictions of three kinds, to which mortals are subject: 1) those caused by one's own body (adhyatmika), 2) those caused by beings around him (adhibhautika), and 3) those caused by devas (adhidaivika).

Taraka: Deliverer.

Taraka Mantra: From the root word *tara*–that which crosses. The Taraka Mantra is that which enables its invokers to cross over the ocean of samsara and attain liberation.

Taraka Nama: The Delivering Name.

Tarakajnana: The knowledge that leads to moksha.

Tarana: Liberation; crossing over Samsara.

Tarka: Reasoning; argumentation; logic; debate.

Tarkashastra: Another name for the Nyaya school; the science of reasoning.

Tarpana: Libation of water for gratifying the manes.

Tat Twam Asi: "Thou art That." The Mahavakya (Great Saying) of the Chandogya Upanishad.

Tattwa: "Thatness." Principle; element; the essence of things; truth; reality.

Tattwa jnana: Knowledge of Brahman; same as Brahmajnana.

Tattvatita: Beyond the elements.

Tattvavit: Knower of the essence of things; sage or Brahmajnani.

Tejas: Radiance; brilliancy (especially spiritual); the element of fire; Agni; heat.

Tejomaya: Full of tejas; full of light; resplendent.

Thakur: "Master" or "Lord." A reference to God or to a holy person considered to be one with God.

Tilak: A sacred mark made on the forehead or between the eyebrows denoting what form of God the person worships.

Tirtha: A sacred place of pilgrimage; a river or body of water in which it is auspicious and spiritually beneficial to bathe; the water offered in ritual worship and then sprinkled on or drunk by the devotees. Also, a name of a Dasanami

Sannyasin belonging to the Dwarka Math.

Titiksha: Endurance of opposites; forbearance; tolerance; the ability to withstand opposites like pleasure and pain, heat and cold, etc., with equal fortitude; the bearing of all afflictions without caring to change them and without anxiety or lament.

Tivra: Intense.

Tivra Mumukshutva: Intense, earnest and consuming desire for liberation (moksha).

Tola: Three-eights of an ounce.

Trailanga Swami: One of the most renowned and miraculous yogis of the nineteenth century, who was over three hundred and fifty years old. He lived during the latter years of his life in Varanasi (Benares).

Trataka: Steady gazing; the process of fixing the gaze on a small dot, point, yantra, etc.

Treta Yuga: See Yuga.

Triguna: The three gunas or qualities: sattwa, rajas, and tamas. (See the entry under Guna).

Trigunamayi: A connotative name of God as the Divine Mother suggesting that She possesses the three gunas.

Trigunatita: Beyond the three gunas.

Trikalajnana: Knowledge of the past, present and the future.

Trikalajnani: One who knows the past, present and the future.

Trikuta: The space between the eyebrows.

Trimurti: "The three forms"–Brahma, Vishnu, and Shiva, the Hindu "Trinity."

Tripti: Satisfaction.

Triputa: The triad (seer, sight, seen).
Triputi: "The triple form." The triad of: knowing, knower, and object known; cognizer, object, and cognition; seer, sight, and seen.
Trishna: Thirst; craving; desire.
Trishula: Trident; weapon wielded by Lord Shiva.
Triveni: The confluence of the three sacred rivers: Ganges, Jumna (Yamuna), and Saraswati, located outside the sacred city of Rudraprayag (called Allahabad in modern times). Considered the most auspicious place for purificatory bathing. The space between the eyebrows.
Tukaram: A poet-saint of seventeenth century India (Maharashtra) devoted to Krishna in his form of Panduranga (Vittala).
Tulasi (Tulsi): The Indian basil plant sacred to Vishnu. Considered a manifestation of the goddess Lakshmi. Its leaves are used in worship of Vishnu and his avataras, and its stems and roots are formed into rosary beads used for counting the repetition of the mantras of Vishnu and his avataras. The leaves of tulasi are also used for purification and even medicinally.
Turiya: The state of pure consciousness. *A Ramakrishna-Vedanta Wordbook* defines it as: "The superconscious; lit., 'the Fourth,' in relation to the three ordinary states of consciousness–waking, dreaming, and dreamless sleep–which it transcends."
Turiya-Turiya: "The consciousness of Consciousness;" the Absolute Consciousness of God, the Consciousness behind

our individualized consciousness (turiya).

Tushti: Contentment; satisfaction.

Tyaga: Literally" leaving; separation; abandonment; renunciation in the sense of dissociation of the mind from worldly objects and the seeds of desire; in the Gita, the relinquishment of the fruit of action.

Tyagi: A renouncer, an ascetic.

U

Uchchaishravas: The name of Indra's horse (or the horse of the Sun god, Surya), that was born of the amrita that was churned from the ocean by the gods. The name means "high-sounding" and refers to the power of mantra.

Uchchishta[m]: The remnants of food eaten by others, the actual leavings from someone's plate, considered extremely unclean physically and psychically. (This does not apply to food left in a serving dish or cooking vessel unless someone ate from it rather than serving it on their own dish.)

Udana: The prana which brings up or carries down what has been drunk or eaten; the general force of assimilation.

Udasina: Indifferent.

Udasinata: Indifference (to objects and sense-attractions); state of being indifferent.

Udbhuta: Such as can be comprehended by the senses; born (out of the elements).

Udbodhaka: Stimulus; awakener.

Uddharsha: Excessive joy.

Udghata: Awakening of the Kundalini Shakti that is lying dormant in the Muladhara chakra.

Udgitha: The Pranava, Om, when it is sung aloud in Vedic recitation.

Uma: See Parvati.

Unmadana: Intoxication, maddening.

Unmana: "That which transcends the mind;" the "mindless" state of a yogi that is really the state beyond the mind.

Unmani: One who is in the state of unmana.

Upadana: Material.

Upadesha: Spiritual instruction; the instructions given by the guru at the time of initiation; initiation itself.

Upadhi: Adjunct; association; superimposed thing or attribute that veils and gives a colored view of the substance beneath it; limiting adjunct; instrument; vehicle; body; a technical term used in Vedanta philosophy for any superimposition that gives a limited view of the Absolute and makes It appear as the relative.

Upaharana: Bringing near; fetching; taking; seizing.

Upalabdhi: Perception; knowledge; attainment.

Upalabdhri: The perceiving or knowing subject.

Upanayana(m): Investure with the sacred thread (yajnopavita) and initiation into the Gayatri mantra.

Upanishads: Books (of varying lengths) of the philosophical teachings of the ancient sages of India on the knowledge of Absolute Reality. The upanishads contain two major themes: (1) the individual self (atman) and the Supreme Self (Paramatman) are one in essence, and (2) the goal of life is the realization/manifestation of this unity, the realization of God (Brahman). There are eleven principal upanishads: Isha, Kena, Katha, Prashna, Mundaka, Mandukya, Taittiriya, Aitareya, Chandogya, Brihadaranyaka, and Shvetashvatara, all of which were commented on by Shankara, Ramanuja and Madhavacharya, thus setting the seal of authenticity on them.

Uparama: Satiety; Vairagya; renunciation of actions.

Uparamata: Calmness of mind; cessation of action.

Uparati: Uparati is the power–once the sense have been restricted–to ensure that they may not once again be drawn toward worldly objects; indifference toward the enjoyment of sense-objects; surfeit; discontinuance of religious ceremonies following upon renunciation; absolute calmness; tranquillity; renunciation.

Upasaka: One who does Upasana; worshipper.

Upasana: "Sitting near" or "drawing near;" worship; adoration; contemplation of God or deity; devout meditation; both teaching and learning.

Upasanamarti: That form of God chosen for worship.

Upasarga: Obstacle.

Upastambaka: Instrumental cause; supporting; encouraging.

Upaya: Means or device.

Upeksha[nam]: Indifference; equanimity resulting from disinterestedness.

Urdhvareta yogi: A yogi in whom the subtle (including sexual) energies flow upwards.

Urdhvaretas: The state of being an urdhvareta yogi; one who is an urdhvareta yogi.

Urmi: A wave; an evil; reference is often made to six evils; they are hunger and thirst, old age and death, grief and delusion or loss of consciousness.

Ushanas: An ancient seer and poet.

Ushmapas: A class of ancestors (pitris) which live off subtle emanations or vapors.

Utkranti: Departure of the soul from the body.

Utpatti: Origin; creation.

Utsaha: Cheerfulness; enthusiasm.

Utsava: Festival; celebration.

Utsava murti: The image of a deity that is taken out in procession rather than the main image in the temple which is usually permanently affixed to a stone pedestal.

Uttama: Best.

Uttamapurusha: Highest person; God.

Uttamarahasya: Highest secret of things.

Uttarayana: The six months of the year, corresponding approximately to the time from January, 15th, to July, 15th; six months of the northern solstice.

V

Vach/Vak: Speech.
Vachaka: That which is denoted by speech.
Vachya/Vakya: That which is denoted by speech.
Vaikhari: Sound that is spoken and heard.
Vaikuntha: The celestial abode (loka) of Vishnu and His devotees.
Vairagi: A renunciate.
Vairagya: Non-attachment; detachment; dispassion; absence of desire; disinterest; or indifference. Indifference towards and disgust for all worldly things and enjoyments.
Vaishnava: A devotee of Vishnu.
Vaishwanara: Universal Being; the Self of the waking state; the sum-total of the created beings; Brahman in the form of the universe; Cosmic Fire; the god of fire; the digestive fire; the gastric fire; the sum-total of the created beings; Brahma in the form of the universe; Virat-purusha.
Vaishya: A member of the merchant, farmer, artisan, businessman caste.
Vaitrishnya: Non-attachment; cravinglessness.

Vajra: Diamond; adamantine firmness; thunderbolt–the special weapon of Indra, king of the gods.

Vak: Speech.

Vaksiddhi: Perfection in speech, in which state whatever one speaks turns out to be true; the result of observance of truthfulness.

Vakya: Word or statement.

Vama: Dear; pleasant; lovely; beautiful; charming; a title of Shiva; left side; opposite; reverse.

Vamana Avatara/Vamanadeva: An incarnation of Vishnu in the Treta Yuga as a Brahmin dwarf.

Vanaprastha: Literally: a forest dweller. The third stage of life (ashrama) in which, leaving home and children, the husband and wife dwell together in seclusion and contemplation as a preparation to taking sannyasa.

Vanchana: Cheating.

Vanhi: Fire.

Vani: Speech; voice; sound; music; language; words.

Varanasi: The most holy city of India, called by Yogananda "the Hindu Jerusalem." Located on the Ganges and dedicated to Shiva (Vishwanatha), it is believed that anyone who dies there will be liberated.

Varna: Caste. (Literally: color.) In traditional Hindu society there were four divisions or castes according to the individual's nature and aptitude: Brahmin, Kshatriya, Vaishya, and Shudra.

Varnashrama: Related to the four castes and the four stages (ashramas) of Hindu life; the laws of caste and ashrama.

Varnashram dharma: The observance of caste and ashram.

Varshneya: Clansman of the Vrishnis–a title of Krishna.

Varuna: A Vedic deity considered the sustainer of the universe and also the presiding deity of the oceans and water. Often identified with the conscience.

Vasana: Subtle desire; a tendency created in a person by the doing of an action or by experience; it induces the person to repeat the action or to seek a repetition of the experience; the subtle impression in the mind capable of developing itself into action; it is the cause of birth and experience in general; an aggregate or bundle of samskaras–the impressions of actions that remain unconsciously in the mind.

Vasana(s): A bundle or aggregate of such samskaras.

Vasanakshaya: Annihilation of subtle desires and impressions.

Vasanarahita: Without subtle desires.

Vasanatyaga: Renunciation of subtle desires.

Vasava: A name of Indra.

Vashikara: Mastery; control (especially complete control); power.

Vashishtha: One of the most famous of Vedic seers (rishis).

Vastu: Object; substance; Brahman,

Vasudeva: "He who dwells in all things"–the Universal God; the father of Krishna, who is himself also sometimes called Vasudeva.

Vasuki: The king of the serpents. He assisted at the churning of the milk ocean.

Vasus: Eight Vedic deities characterized by radiance.

Vasyata: Mastery; control; obedience.

Vatsalya: The attitude of a devotee expressing parental relationship with God, looking upon Him as a child.

Vayu: The Vedic god of the wind; air; vital breath; Prana.

Veda: Knowledge, wisdom, revealed scripture. See Vedas.

Vedanashakti: Power of cognition or sensation.

Vedanga: An auxiliary to the Vedas. The Vedangas are six in number:

1. Shiksha–the science of proper articulation and pronunciation.
2. Kalpa–Rituals and ceremonies.
3. Vyakarana–Grammar.
4. Nirukta–Etymological explanation of different Vedic words.
5. Chandas–The science of prosody.
6. Jyotisha–Astronomy, astrology.

Vedanta: Literally, "the end of the Vedas;" the Upanishads; the school of Hindu thought, based primarily on the Upanishads, upholding the doctrine of either pure non-dualism or conditional non-dualism. The original text of this school is Vedanta-darshana, the Brahma Sutras compiled by the sage Vyasa.

Vedanta Sutras: The Brahma Sutras.

Vedantin: A follower of Vedanta.

Vedas: The oldest scriptures of India, considered the oldest scriptures of the world, that were revealed in meditation to the Vedic Rishis (seers). Although in modern times there are said to be four Vedas (Rig, Sama, Yajur, and Atharva), in the upanishads only three are listed (Rig, Sama, and Yajur). In actuality, there is only one Veda: the Rig Veda. The Sama Veda is only a collection of Rig Veda hymns that are marked (pointed) for singing. The Yajur Veda is a small book giving directions on just one form of Vedic sacrifice. The Atharva Veda is only a collection of theurgical mantras to be recited for the cure of various afflictions or to be recited over the herbs to be taken as medicine for those afflictions.

Vedic: Having to do with the Vedas.

Vega: Motion; velocity; force; inertia.

Vibhaga: Division.

Vibhu: All-pervading; great.

Vibhuti: Manifestations of divine power or glory; the special forms in which the Lord reveals himself; might; prosperity; welfare; splendor; exalted rank; greatness; miraculous powers; superhuman power resembling that of God (Ishwara). The quality of all-pervasiveness (omnipresence). Also sacred ash from a fire sacrifice.

Vichara: Subtle thought; reflection; enquiry; introspection; investigation; enquiry/investigation into the nature of the Self, Brahman or Truth; ever-present reflection on the why and wherefore of things; enquiry into the real meaning of the Mahavakya Tat-twam-asi: Thou art That; discrimination between the Real and the unreal; enquiry of Self.

Vicharashakti: Power of enquiry.

Videha: Bodiless.

Videhakaivalya mukti: Disembodied salvation.

Videhamukti: Disembodied salvation; salvation attained by the realized soul after shaking off the physical sheath as opposed to jivanmukti which is liberation even while living.

Videhi: One who is bodiless.
Vidhi: Injunction; method; rule.
Vidhiparvaka: In accordance with the scriptural injunctions.
Vidvan: A knowing person; the term is particularly applied to one that knows the real nature of the Self as distinct from the body; an expert in all aspects of the Sanskrit language.
Vidvat sannyasa: Renunciation after the attainment of the knowledge of Brahman. Asceticism resorted to by the wise (jnanis) and perfected ones (siddhas). Renunciation by the wise. Sannyas conferred without the elaborate rituals–either simply with some mantras or with none but the giving of the gerua cloth and bestowal of a sannyas name.
Vidya: Knowledge; both spiritual knowledge and mundane knowledge.
Vidyapith(a): "Seat of knowledge;" school.
Vighna: Obstacle.
Vighnesha: The god who removes obstacles; same as Ganesha, son of Lord Shiva.
Vijara: Ageless; without old age.
Vijaya: Victory; triumph.
Vijnana: The highest knowledge, beyond mere theoretical knowledge (jnana); transcendental knowledge or knowing; experiential knowledge; a high state of spiritual realization–intimate knowledge of God in which all is seen as manifestations of Brahman; knowledge of the Self.
Vijnanamayakosha: One of the sheaths of the soul consisting of the principle, intellect or Buddhi.
Vijnanaspandita: Movement of consciousness.

Vijnanatma: Cognitional Self; soul-intellectual Self.

Vijnani: One endowed with vijnana.

Vikalpa: Imagination; fantasy; mental construct; abstraction; conceptualization; hallucination; distinction; experience; thought; oscillation of the mind.

Vikara: Change, change of form, or modification–generally with reference to the modification of the mind, individually or cosmically.; gluiness; manifestation.

Vikasa: State of expansion, as in evolution of the world.

Vikarshanashakti: Power of repulsion.

Vikrita: Changed; modified; ready or prone to create.

Vikriti: Change; derivative products of Prakriti, as Mahat, Buddhi, mind, the senses and the Tanmatr-as.

Vikshepa: The projecting power of the mind, causing external involvement; the movement of pushing outward or away; the projecting power of ignorance; mental restlessness resulting from the awareness moving out from the center that is the Self; Distractions; causes of distractions; projection; false projection; the tossing of the mind which obstructs concentration.

Vikshepashakti: The power of Maya that projects the universe and causes movement and superimposition.

Vikshipta: Distracted; scattered; not collected.

Vilwa: See Bel.

Vimala: Purity; unblemished; without stain or defect.

Vimarsha: Consideration; examination; test; reasoning; discussion; knowledge; intelligence; reflection; dissatisfaction; displeasure; impatience.

Vinasha: Destruction.

Vinashi: Perishable.

Vinaya: Humility or sense of propriety; manners; education; mental culture and refinement.

Viniyoga: Application.

Vipaka: A type of transformation; ripening; resultant; fruition.

Viparita: Contrary; perverted.

Viparitabhavana: Wrong conception, such as conceiving the body as the Self; perverted understanding or imagination.

Viparitata: Dissimilarity in objects; reversion.

Viparyaya: Erroneous cognition; wrong knowledge; illusion; misapprehension; distraction of mind.

Vipra: Inspired; wise, gifted with superior insight; sage; seer; priest; Brahmin.

Viraha: Burning agony due to the separation from the Lord.

Viraj: The macrocosm; the manifested universe; the world man–the masculine potency in nature in contradistinction to the feminine potency.

Viraja: Free from Rajas or passion; a river which has to be crossed before the world of Brahma is to be reached and which only eminent and saintly men, devoid of passion and desire can cross.

Viraja homa: "Universal homa;" the final fire sacrifice done just before taking sannyas in which offerings are made to all living beings in petition for their releasing of the prospective sannyasin from all karmic obligations he might have in relation to them.

Virakti: Same as Vairagya.

Virasa: Without essence.

Virat: Macrocosm; the cosmic form of the Self as the cause of the gross world; the all-pervading Spirit in the form of the universe.

Viratpurusha: The deity presiding over the universe; the cosmic or universal aspect of the deity.

Virochana: King of the demons (asuras). According to the Chandogya Upanishad, along with Indra he went to the Creator to learn the nature of the Self. Misunderstanding the teaching: "Virochana, satisfied for his part that he had found out the Self, returned to the demons and began to teach them that the body alone is to be worshiped, that the body alone is to be served, and that he who worships the body and serves the body gains both worlds, this and the next."

Virodhat: Opposition; conflict; contradiction.

Virya: Strength; power; energy; courage; seminal energy.

Visarjana: Removal; the final item in Upasana or worship by which the worshipper devotedly prays to the divine presence invoked in the idol, to return to its original abode.

Vishada: Sadness; dejection.

Vishaya (1): Object; object of perception (sensory experience) or enjoyment; subject matter; content; areas; range; field-object domain; sphere; realm, scope; matters of enjoyment or experience.

Vishaya (2): Doubt.

Vishayabhoga: Sensual enjoyment.

Vishayachaitanya: Consciousness as objects; the object known;

the consciousness determined by the object cognized.

Vishayakara: Of the form of the objects perceived; the condition of the mind in perception.

Vishayashakti: Attachment to sensual objects.

Vishayasamsara: Objective or sensual world.

Vishayavritti: Thought of sensual objects.

Vishayavrittipravaha: The continuous thought-current of worldly objects; the flow of objective thinking.

Vishesha: Special; distinctive qualification; distinguishable; particularity; propriety.

Visheshaguna: Special quality.

Visheshajnana: Special knowledge; detailed knowledge.

Visheshana: Attribute; property; an invariable and distinguishing attribute; specification.

Visheshavastha: Differentiated condition.

Visheshavijnana: Special knowledge; knowledge of the Self, as opposed to the knowledge of phenomenal science.

Vishishta: Complex; qualified.

Vishishtadvaita Vedanta: The philosophy of Qualified Non-Dualism formulated by Sri Ramanuja.

Vishoka: Blissful; serene; free of grief, suffering or sorrow.

Vishnu: "The all-pervading;" God as the Preserver.

Vishnugranthi: The knot of ignorance at the Manipura chakra.

Vishnumaya: Illusion wielded by the Supreme Lord so that the unreal seems real; the illusory form of Lord Vishnu usually conceived of as a female deity which makes the universe appear as real.

Vishuddha: Supremely pure; totally pure.

Vishuddha chakra: "Supreme purity." Energy center located in the spine opposite the hollow of the throat. Seat of the Ether element.

Vishuddhi: Supreme purity; total purity.

Vishwa: Cosmos; a name of the Jiva in the waking state.

Vishwa devas: A group of twelve minor Vedic deities.

Vishwanatha: "Lord of the Universe;" a title of Shiva, often applied to his temple in Varanasi (Benares).

Vishwaprana: The universal life force (prana).

Vishwarupa: Cosmic form; multiform having all forms.

Vishwasa: Faith.

Vismriti: Loss of memory; forgetfulness.

Vistara: Expansion.

Vitanda: Cavilling; idle carping; a frivolous or fallacious argument or commentary.

Vitaraga: Free from attachment (raga); one who has abandoned desire/attachment; a sannyasi.

Vitarka: Thought; reasoning; cogitation with sense perception; discussion; debate; logical argument.

Vithoba: See Vitthala.

Vittaishana: Desire for wealth.

Vitthala: A title of Krishna, meaning "the one standing on a brick," a reference to the image of Krishna worshipped in Pandharpur in Western India.

Vivarta: Illusory appearance; a doctrine of the Nondualistic school of Vedanta philosophy explaining creation as an illusory appearance of the Absolute; apparent variation; illusory manifestation of Brahman; apparent or unreal or seeming change; superimposition; appearance.

Vivartashristi: Creation where the original reality remains what it is and yet apparently brings about the effect, according to Advaita school of thought.

Vivartavada: Phenomenalism. See Vivarta.

Vivartopadana: A material cause which does not undergo the slightest substantial change in the production of the effect, but presents an inseparable phenomenal effect. It is opposed to Parinami Upadana, which is actually transformed into the effect. Brahman is Vivartopadana of the universe according to Sri Sankara. A piece of rope is mistaken for a snake. This is an example of Vivartopadana. A fictitious material cause is Vivartopadana.

Viveka: Discrimination between the Real and the unreal, between the Self and the non-Self, between the permanent and the impermanent; right intuitive discrimination.

Viveka-purvaka-vairagya: Vairagya arising from discrimination (viveka) between the real and the unreal.

Vivekananda (Swami): The chief disciple of Sri Ramakrishna, who brought the message of Vedanta to the West at the end of the nineteenth century.

Viveki(n): One who possesses discrimination (viveka).

Vividisha sannyasa: Renunciation for the purpose of knowing Brahman.

Vrata: Vow; a resolution; rule of conduct.

Vrindavan: See Brindaban.

Vrishnis: The clan to which Krishna belonged.

Vritra: One who hates the light and burrows into the dark;

a symbolic term used in the Vedas for those of low and bound consciousness who are the opposite of the Aryans.

Vritti: Thought-wave; mental modification; mental whirlpool; a ripple in the chitta (mind substance).

Vrittijnana: Secular science; knowledge obtained through the mind; experience of the world.

Vrittilaya: Dissolution of the mental modification.

Vrittisahita: Associated with thought.

Vrittivyapti: The mind assuming the form of objects perceived; pervasion of the psyche.

Vyadhi: Disease of the body.

Vyahriti: The sacred syllables, Bhuh, Bhuvah, Svah.

Vyakta: Manifest(ed); revealed.

Vyaktitva: Personality.

Vyakti-upasana: Meditation on manifested God.

Vyakhyana: Explanation and commentary.

Vyana: The prana that holds prana and apana together and produces circulation in the body.

Vyapaka: All-pervading; all-pervader.

Vyapakatma: All-pervading soul.

Vyapi: One who pervades.

Vyasa: One of the greatest sages of India, commentator on the Yoga Sutras, author of the Mahabharata (which includes the Bhagavad Gita), the Brahma Sutras, and the codifier of the Vedas.

Vyashti: Individual; microcosm.

Vyatireka: Separate; negation.

Vyavahara: Worldly activity; relative activity as opposed to

Absolute Being; empirical/phenomenal world; worldly relation; worldly life which is the basis of all one's practical movements.

Vyavaharapeksha: With a view to the world of appearance or relativity.

Vyavaharika: Practical; phenomenal; empirical; relative.

Vyavaharikasatta: Empirical reality.

Vyavasaya: Settled concentration and perseverance; application; cultivation.

Vyavasayatimka: One with resolution and determination.

Vyoma/Vyomakasha: Ether (akasha); the sky.

Vyutthana: Rising up; awakening; emergence; externalization; outgoing; rising; waking state; a stage in Yoga.

Word-Brahman: Om; Shabda Brahman.

Y

Yadava: "Descendant of Yadu" an ancient Indian king; the Yadavas, a clan of India, were descended from King Yadu; a title of Krishna, since he was part of the Yadava clan. Swami Bhaktivedanta, founder of the Hare Krishna movement in the West, as well as some anthropologists, believed that the Yadava clan, who disappeared from India shortly after Krishna's lifetime, emigrated to the middle east and became the people we know today as the Jews, Abraham having been a Yadava.

Yajna: Sacrifice; offering; sacrificial ceremony; a ritual sacrifice; usually the fire sacrifice known as agnihotra or havan.

Yajnaypitha: See Yajnasthala.

Yajnasthala: An open sided, roofed structure in which the fire sacrifice is performed.

Yajnavalkya: A great sage whose teachings are recorded in the Brihadaranyaka Upanishad; the guru of King Janaka.

Yajnopavita: Sacred thread. A triple thread worn by the twice-born (dwijas) that represents the threefold Brahman. It is essential for the performance of all the rites of the twice-born. Usually worn only by Brahmins, originally it was worn by Kshatriyas and Vaishyas as well.

Yajnopavitin: Wearer of the sacred thread (yajnopavita).

Yaksha: There are two kinds of yakshas: 1) semidivine beings whose king is Kubera, the lord of wealth, or 2) a kind of ghost, goblin, or demon.

Yama (1): Restraint; the five Don'ts of Yoga: 1) ahimsa–non-violence, non-injury, harmlessness; 2) satya–truthfulness, honesty; 3) asteya–non-stealing, honesty, non-misappropriativeness; 4) brahmacharya–continence; 5) aparigraha–non-possessiveness, non-greed, non-selfishness, non-acquisitiveness. These five are called the Great Vow (Observance, Mahavrata) in the Yoga Sutras.

Yama (2): Yamaraja; the Lord of Death, controller of who dies and what happens to them after death.

Yama Duta: A messenger of Yama; who who comes to take the soul from the body at the time of death.

Yamuna: A sacred river, tributary of the Ganges, which flows through Brindaban, the home of Lord Krishna in his childhood.

Yantra: Geometrical designs of the energy patterns made by mantras when they are recited or which, when concentrated on produce the effects of the corresponding mantras. Though often attributed to deities, they are really the diagrams of the energy movements of those deities' mantras.

Yashas: Fame; reputation; glory; renown; honor; beauty; splendor.

Yashoda: The foster-mother of Krishna in Brindaban where

Krishna was taken by his father Vasudeva on the night of his birth for his protection from his mother Devaki's brother, Kansa, the king of Mathura. His foster-father was Nanda.

Yatamana: One who attempts to disallow the mind from running in the sensual grooves; a state of Vairagya.

Yathartha: Real; a things as it really is.

Yathartha swarupa: Essential nature.

Yati: Wanderer; a wandering ascetic.

Yatra: Pilgrimage.

Yatri: Pilgrim.

Yoga: Literally, "joining" or "union" from the Sanskrit root yuj. Union with the Supreme Being, or any practice that makes for such union. Meditation that unites the individual spirit with God, the Supreme Spirit. The name of the philosophy expounded by the sage Patanjali, teaching the process of union of the individual with the Universal Soul.

Yoga Darshana: See Yoga Sutras.

Yoga Marga: The path of meditation and inner purification leading to union with God.

Yoga Shastra: The scriptures and writings of various authorities dealing specifically with the theory and practice of yoga, especially the Yoga Sutras (Yoga Darshan) of Patanjali.

Yoga Siddhi: Spiritual perfection or psychic power resulting from the practice of Yoga.

Yoga Sutras: The oldest known writing on the subject of yoga, written by the sage Patanjali, a yogi of ancient India, and considered the most authoritative text on yoga. Also known as Yoga Darshana, it is the basis of the Yoga

Philosophy which is based on the philosophical system known as Sankhya.

Yoga Vashishtha: A classical treatise on Yoga, containing the instructions of the Rishi Vashishta to Lord Rama on meditation and spiritual life.

Yogabhrashta: One who has fallen from the high state of Yoga.

Yogabhyasa: Practice of Yoga.

Yogadrishti: Yoga-vision.

Yogamaya: The power of Maya, of divine illusion. It is Maya in operation, the operation/movement rising from the presence (union–yoga) of God (Ishwara) within it, and therefore possessing delusive power.

Yogananda (Paramhansa): The most influential yogi of the twentieth century in the West, author of *Autobiography of a Yogi* and founder of Self-Realization Fellowship in America.

Yoga Nidra/Yoganidra: A state of half-contemplation and half-sleep; light yogic sleep when the individual retains slight awareness; state between sleep and wakefulness.

Yoga Siddha: One who is perfected in yoga and therefore totally liberated and united with Brahman.

Yogarudha: One who is established in Yoga.

Yogayukta: One who is established in Yoga or linked up through Yoga.

Yogeshwara: Lord of Yoga; a title of both Shiva and Lord Krishna.

Yogi(n): One who practices Yoga; one who strives earnestly for union with God; an aspirant going through any course of spiritual discipline.

Yogic: Having to do with Yoga.

Yogigamya: Attainable only by a Yogi.

Yogini: A female practicer of yoga.

Yogiraj: "King of Yogis," a title often given to an advanced yogi, especially a teacher of yogi.

Yogyata: Fitness; capability; readiness; ability.

Yojana: A measure of distance said to be equivalent to 9 or 10 miles.

Yoni: Womb; source.

Yuga: Age or cycle; aeon; world era. Hindus believe that there are four yugas: the Golden Age (Satya or Krita Yuga), the Silver age (Treta Yuga), The Bronze Age (Dwapara Yuga), and the Iron Age (Kali Yuga). Satya Yuga is four times as long as the Kali Yuga; Treta Yuga is three times as long; and Dwapara Yuga is twice as long. In the Satya Yuga the majority of humans use the total potential–four-fourths– of their minds; in the Treta Yuga, three-fourths; in the Dwapara Yuga, one half; and in the Kali Yuga, one fourth. (In each Yuga there are those who are using either more or less of their minds than the general populace.) The Yugas move in a perpetual circle: Ascending Kali Yuga, ascending Dwapara Yuga, ascending Treta Yuga, ascending Satya Yuga, descending Satya Yuga, descending, Treta Yuga, descending Dwapara Yuga, and descending Kali Yuga–over and over. Furthermore, there are yuga cycles within yuga cycles. For example, there are yuga cycles that affect the entire cosmos, and smaller yuga cycles within those greater cycles that affect a solar system. The cosmic yuga cycle takes 8,640,000,000 years, whereas the solar yuga cycle only takes 24,000 years. At the present time our solar system is in the ascending Dwapara Yuga, but the cosmos is in the descending Kali Yuga. Consequently, the more the general mind of humanity develops, the more good can be accomplished by the positive, and the more evil can be accomplished by the negative. Therefore we have more contrasts and polarization in contemporary life than previously before 1900.

Yukteswar Giri, Swami Sri: The guru of Paramhansa Yogananda.

Yukti (1): Union or Yoga.

Yukti (2): Reasoning (about something); skill; cleverness; device.

Did you enjoy reading this book?

Thank you for taking the time to read *A Brief Sanskrit Glossary*. If you enjoyed it, please consider telling your friends or posting a short review at Amazon.com, Goodreads, or the site of your choice.

Word of mouth is an author's best friend and much appreciated.

Get your FREE Meditation Guide

Sign up for the Light of the Spirit Newsletter and get *Ten Simple Tips to Improve Your Meditation Today.*

Get free updates: newsletters, blog posts, and podcasts, plus exclusive content from Light of the Spirit Monastery.

Visit: http://ocoy.org/newsletter-registration

About the Author

Abbot George Burke (Swami Nirmalananda Giri) is the founder and director of the Light of the Spirit Monastery (Atma Jyoti Ashram) in Cedar Crest, New Mexico, USA.

In his many pilgrimages to India, he had the opportunity of meeting some of India's greatest spiritual figures, including Swami Sivananda of Rishikesh and Anandamayi Ma. During his first trip to India he was made a member of the ancient Swami Order by Swami Vidyananda Giri, a direct disciple of Paramhansa Yogananda, who had himself been given sannyas by the Shankaracharya of Puri, Jagadguru Bharati Krishna Tirtha.

In the United States he also encountered various Christian saints, including Saint John Maximovich of San Francisco and Saint Philaret Voznesensky of New York. He was ordained in the Liberal Catholic Church (International) to the priesthood on January 25, 1974, and consecrated a bishop on August 23, 1975.

For many years Abbot George has researched the identity of Jesus Christ and his teachings with India and Sanatana Dharma, including Yoga. It is his conclusion that Jesus lived in

India for most of his life, and was a yogi and Sanatana Dharma missionary to the West. After his resurrection he returned to India and lived the rest of his life in the Himalayas.

He has written extensively on these and other topics, many of which are posted at OCOY.org.

Light of the Spirit Monastery

Light of the Spirit Monastery is an esoteric Christian monastic community for those men who seek direct experience of the Spirit through meditation, sacramental worship, discipline and dedicated communal life, emphasizing the inner reality of "Christ in you the hope of glory," as taught by the illumined mystics of East and West.

The public outreach of the monastery is through its website, OCOY.org (Original Christianity and Original Yoga). There you will find many articles on Original Christianity and Original Yoga, including *Esoteric Christian Beliefs*. *Foundations of Yoga* and *How to Be a Yogi* are practical guides for anyone seriously interested in living the Yoga Life.

You will also discover many other articles on leading an effective spiritual life, including *The Yoga of the Sacraments* and *Spiritual Benefits of a Vegetarian Diet*, as well as the "Dharma for Awakening" series—in-depth commentaries on these spiritual classics: the Upanishads, the Bhagavad Gita, and the Tao Teh King.

You can listen to a series of podcasts by Abbot George on meditation, the Yoga Life, and remarkable spiritual people he has met in India and elsewhere, at http://ocoy.org/podcasts/

Reading for Awakening

Light of the Spirit Press presents books on spiritual wisdom and Original Christianity and Original Yoga. From our "Dharma for Awakening" series (practical commentaries on the world's scriptures) to books on how to meditate and live a successful spiritual life, you will find books that are informative, helpful, and even entertaining.

Light of the Spirit Press is the publishing house of Light of the Spirit Monastery (Atma Jyoti Ashram) in Cedar Crest, New Mexico, USA. Our books feature the writings of the founder and director of the monastery, Abbot George Burke (Swami Nirmalananda Giri) which are also found on the monastery's website, OCOY.org.

We invite you to explore our publications in the following pages.

Find out more about our publications at
lightofthespiritpress.com

Discover books on Meditation

Soham Yoga: *the Yoga of the Self*

This Soham meditation has been the most simple, effective kind of meditation I have practiced. Everything one needs to learn and practice Soham meditation is in this book. It is a treasure. —*Arnold Van Wie*

Om Yoga Meditation: *Its Theory and Practice*

Om Yoga Meditation uniquely touches on the spiritual power and lasting positive effects of the mantra Om. If you're curious about trying the mantra Om in your spiritual practice, this book is the perfect guide with theory and techniques to help you along the way. —*Spirituality & Health Magazine*

Read the "Dharma for Awakening" Series

The Dhammapada for Awakening
A Commentary on Buddha's Practical Wisdom

I intend to read it over and over again. There is no modern scholar who in my opinion has a better grasp of these topics than Abbot George.—*Tachira*

The Gospel of Thomas for Awakening
A Commentary on Jesus' Sayings as Recorded by the Apostle Thomas

As informed and informative as it is inspired and inspiring.—*Midwest Book Review*

The Bhagavad Gita for Awakening
A Practical Commentary for Leading a Successful Spiritual Life

It is clear, helpful, and has a vast depth that easily brings both the meaning and value of the Bhagavad Gita to life.—*Michael Sabani*

More from Light of the Spirit Press

the CHRIST of INDIA

The "Lost Years" and much more

over 40 ★★★★★ reviews

The Christ of India: *The Story of Original Christianity*

It illuminates the life of Jesus in an enlarged context beyond religion that makes it a spiritual page-turner.—*Rev. Gerry Nangle*

Satsang with the Abbot: *Questions and Answers about Life, Spiritual Liberty, and the Pursuit of Ultimate Happiness*

This is the most insightful and interesting book I have read for a long time, maybe ever! —*Alan Dawe*

Dwelling in the Mirror: *A Study of Illusions Produced by Delusive Meditation and How to Be Free from Them*

I urge anyone who is just starting on their path to read this book as it will help separate the "gold" from the "dross". —*Marie-Angele*

Robe of Light: *An Esoteric Christian Cosmology*

Great book for Christians and Non-Christians alike to re-evaluate their outlook on the Universe and to question their own role in it. —*Batto*

May a Christian Believe in Reincarnation?

The overall best book I have read on reincarnation and Christianity. I highly recommend it. —*J. W. Stansell*

The Bhagavad Gita - The Song of God

A must have, for anyone studying Dharma (a way of life that supports meditation). —*Michael Maldonado*

Spiritual Benefits of a Vegetarian Diet

The information provided in the *Spiritual Benefits of a Vegetarian Diet* makes abundantly clear the subtle energetic effects and benefits of a plant-based diet. —*Devi Spring*

Foundations of Yoga: *Ten Important Principles Every Meditator Should Know*

Coming in the near future:

The Upanishads for Awakening:
A Practical Commentary for Effective Spirituality

The Yoga Sutras for Awakening:
A Practical Commentary on Patanjali's Yoga Sutras

www.ingramcontent.com/pod-product-compliance
Lightning Source LLC
Chambersburg PA
CBHW051649040426
42446CB00009B/1050